Beaded
dimensional embroidery

HELAN PEARCE

SALLYMILNER
PUBLISHING

First published in 2004 by
Sally Milner Publishing Pty Ltd
PO Box 2104
Bowral NSW 2576
AUSTRALIA

Design: Anna Warren, Warren Ventures
Editing: Carol Natsis
Photography: Neil Lorimer
Illustrations: Wendy Gorton

Printed in China

National Library of Australia Cataloguing-in-Publication data

Pearce, Helan.
    Beaded dimensional embroidery.
    ISBN 1 86351 326 4.
    1. Bead embroidery - Patterns. I. Title.
    746.5

Disclaimer
The information in this instruction book is presented in good faith. However, no warranty is given, nor results guaranteed, nor is freedom from any patent to be inferred. Since we have no control over the use of the information contained in this book, the publisher and the author disclaim liability for untoward results.

10 9 8 7 6 5 4 3 2 1

Inside front cover: *Masquerade*.

Cover: *Cornucopia*, with *Luxuriant leaves* detail behind

ontents

Pattern sheet (in back pocket)

A Twisted vine

B Christmas stocking

C Old-fashioned Santa skirt

D Old-fashioned Santa overskirt

E Old-fashioned Santa sleeve

F Old-fashioned Santa hat

Introduction

This is my second book and it was just as much of a challenge as the first. My original idea was to include new designs for flowers similar to those in *Dimensional Embroidery*, but I also began to work on incorporating my love of beading into embroidery using wiring techniques. As a result, I have further developed my dimensional techniques to include beads, creating a completely new effect.

The projects and designs reflect my love of sixteenth- and seventeenth-century embroidery. The designs are small and can be achieved relatively quickly. They can be used in a number of ways — as hair ornaments, on evening bags, on clothing, as home décor accessories and even as Christmas ornaments. The photographs of the projects and the accompanying instructions incorporate the colour schemes I chose when making them, but you may wish to experiment with different colours to suit your own taste and décor.

The beading on and amongst the embroidery lends sparkle and glamour to each piece. You can add more or fewer beads, depending on how you intend to use each design. You can never have too many beads! They add texture and dimension to every piece of work. One of my students beaded an Advent calendar that I had designed and it was so heavy with beads that I think she had to have the lounge room wall reinforced before she could hang it up!

I have been beading for twelve years and teaching embroidery for about twenty-five years. My students have put into practice all the dimensional techniques that I have developed. They often start beading designs for the following Christmas as early as February and each year they are looking for new projects.

My husband frequently asks me, 'Don't you ever get fed up with sewing?' and my answer is always 'No!' For me it is a relaxation and I still enjoy it immensely, especially the challenge of creating new and different designs. And now that I no longer have children at home, I am able to devote more time to my sewing.

My next challenge is to make my daughter's wedding dress and the bridesmaids' dresses — of course they will all be beaded.

I do hope you enjoy the projects in this book as much as I have enjoyed developing the designs for them.

HELAN PEARCE

Materials

Beading needles

Most beading needles are long and fine — I use size 10 or 12. If you find these hard to thread, try big eye needles. Instead of an eye at one end, they have a slit in the centre, which makes threading easier. You can also buy short beading needles.

Embroidery needles

- For fine wool, use a size 7 crewel needle.
- For fine silk, when using one or two strands, use a size 8 crewel needle.
- For the thicker threads, use chenille needles.
- For metallic threads and quilting, use quilting needles.

Beading thread

- Any of the many different brands of beading threads available are suitable for the projects in this book. Use a D or medium-weight thread.
- Not all coloured threads are colour-fast — always check before using.
- For a cream or light-coloured fabric, use either a cream or light-grey thread.
- For a dark-coloured fabric, use a thread to match the fabric.
- Sew gold beads with a grey thread.
- You can wax thread to prevent it from knotting as you work, but take care not to over-wax as this may mark the fabric.

Embroidery threads

I have used a wide range of silk, rayon and cotton threads, a variety of wools, and silk ribbon. Do not cut the threads too long, or they will twist and fray.

Beads

- The quantities given for each project should be sufficient. If you think you are likely to lose some, or the cat, dog or children may knock them over, you may need to allow more!
- I have used size 11 Delica beads. They are sold as DBR (Delica Bead Round), DBC (Delica Bead Cut) or DBL (Delica Bead Large). The colour is indicated by the number that follows the abbreviation: e.g. DBR 678 is Delica Bead Round in mid-pink.
- When using coloured seed beads, check that they are colour-fast.
- Two-cut beads are glass beads that sparkle, but they are available in only a few colours.
- You can vary the types and colours of beads and crystals used in the projects to suit your own taste or if you cannot obtain the ones I have used—it really doesn't matter.
- Glass faceted beads are cheaper than hand-cut beads.
- The letters AB following the name indicate that the beads reflect the light and sparkle, giving a rainbow effect.
- Some suppliers of crystal, glass, bugle and pearl beads are listed at the back of the book. The beads are also available by mail order.
- Names and codes used for crystal beads can vary according to the supplier.

Fabrics

- A firm silk satin (called dynasty or queen silk) or dupion silk is used for most of the projects in this book. The softness of these fabrics makes them a pleasure to work with and enhances the embroidery.
- To make the leaves and petals in some of the designs, I use Vilene, a non-woven interfacing that comes in different thicknesses. Thin Vilene tends to tear when working, so use medium or thick.
- A light-weight woven interfacing (Shapewell or Permashape) in white or black is used as a backing for most projects to stabilise the embroidery and beading. The heaviest weight is difficult to work with, so make sure you choose a light or medium weight.
- An acrylic felt is used to back the shaped designs. This is sold in cut squares or by the metre in a variety of colours. Always check colour-fastness before using.
- A natural felt is used as backing for the *Splendid slipper*, as this is much firmer than the acrylic felt and stands up to a lot of handling when embroidering and beading.
- For *Masquerade*, buckram (a very stiff fabric) is used inside the mask to hold it in shape.

Soluweb

Soluweb is a light-weight stabiliser that dissolves in water. It is useful either for tracing designs (especially for use with dark fabrics) or to form extensions of leaves or petals.

How to use

1 Use a waterproof marking pen to trace the design onto the soluweb.
2 Tack the soluweb with the traced design onto the right side of the fabric.
3 Embroider through all thicknesses (the soluweb, fabric and any backing).
4 For extensions to petals or leaves, pin the work right side up onto the soluweb and then work the stitching.
5 When the embroidery is finished, place your work in a bowl of cold water and leave for about 20 minutes. Never run cold water onto the embroidery from the tap, as this can damage the threads.
6 Change the water and repeat to check that there is no residue left behind.

My students have used soluweb for beading projects on velvet with no adverse effects when dissolved properly. It is safe to use with the fabrics specified for projects in this book, but if you use different fabrics, make sure you test the process before embarking on the work.

Padding

• Pellon is a light-weight fabric used to pad designs that require quilting or to back a picture before it is framed.
• A soft, light-weight wadding is used for the *Old-fashioned Santa*. If you cannot find this, use three layers of Pellon.

Wires

Beading wire is suitable for most of the designs in this book. It must be tarnish-free. The gauge used depends on the shape of the design and is specified for each project. For fine leaf details or small petals, use a fine wire — either 30-gauge green-covered wire, 28-gauge beading wire or 8 amp fuse wire.

For most of the projects, the wire is couched on the wrong side of the Vilene.

Felt backing

Two pieces of felt backing are used. One piece is used to sandwich the thicker wire and beading. The second piece of felt is cut slightly larger than the embroidered and beaded shapes, since the cut felt tends to shrink a little. Cutting it slightly larger leaves enough felt to pick up with your needle when whip stitching the beads around the outside of the shape.

Pens

- Trace designs using a blue water-erasable pen or a fine waterproof pen. Instructions are given in individual projects for removing the blue water-erasable pen.
- Markers are useful for touching up the white Vilene around the edges of leaves, especially in the *Summer berries* design. Copic has a good range of colours.

Tips and techniques

General beading hints

- For easy access, place beads on a piece of velvet to the right of your work if you are right-handed or to the left if you are left-handed.
- Always work in a good light.
- Use single thread for most of the projects in this book, except when securing crystals or glass beads, which need double thread.
- When you are sewing a long length of beads, you can prevent them from coming undone by working a small backstitch through the fabric every now and then to secure them as you go.
- You may find it easier to bead towards you instead of working away from you.
- To start beading, first knot the thread, then bring the needle through to the right side of the fabric and work a small backstitch to stop the knot from popping through the fabric.
- To finish off your thread, weave it through the stitches on the back of your work and secure well.
- Colours shown in beading diagrams are positional only and may differ from the colours of the beads to be used.

Sewing beads in a straight line

- Thread the required number of beads onto your needle, take your needle forward the total length of the beads and working from right to left pick up a small amount of fabric. Pull the needle through so that the beads lie on top of the material.

Whip stitching any combination of beads over two seams or in a straight line

- Use the same technique for small bugle beads, sewing them as though they are small beads.
- If the line of beads is crooked, you are not taking your needle far enough forward: i.e. you are sewing the beads too close together.

Sewing beads around designs

- When whipping beads around the edges of the shapes, use the same technique as for sewing in a straight line. This applies whether you are sewing one bead or groups of three beads.
- Secure the thread, pick up the required number of beads and take your needle forward the length of the beads. Working from right to left, pick up a small amount of material and bring your needle through to the buttonholed edge of the shape. Repeat around the rest of the shape.

Attaching bicones

When attaching crystal bicones, sew them on through the holes in the middle, as shown in diagram (a). Alternatively (diagram b), secure the thread in position, then pick up a bicone and a small Delica bead. Insert the needle back through the bicone hole to the back of the fabric and secure the thread. This technique is also used to attach crystal flowers.

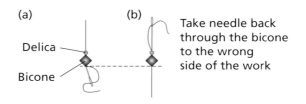

(a)

Delica

Bicone

(b)

Take needle back through the bicone to the wrong side of the work

Embroidery stitches

- The main stitch used for the projects in this book is a closely worked buttonhole stitch, either long or short. This seals the edges of the shapes and allows you to cut away the fabric very close to the stitching. It is important to use this stitch to prevent the fabric from fraying or stitching from coming undone. Always use a small, sharp pair of scissors to cut out the shapes. You will find it easier if you first cut the shapes out roughly and then trim them close to the buttonholed edge.

- Always work any laid stitches first, before embroidering stem or other stitches around the outside or on top of the laidwork.

- If you prefer to add a personal touch to the embroidery, you can use different stitches from those shown.

Stitching and beading symbols

For each design, there are diagrams showing stitches, threads and beading (where relevant). Keys to the symbols are provided with each project.

- In the stitching diagrams, a letter symbol is used to indicate the type of stitch: e.g. in the *Twisted vine* project, A = stem stitch. The letter is followed by a number, which indicates the type of thread used: e.g. A/1 = stem stitch with pale pink thread.

- In the beading diagrams, the type and colour of bead is indicated by a number: e.g. in the *Twisted vine* project, 2 = Delica 672 (cream). The notation 'three of 2' means pick up three Delica 672 beads.

Twisted vine

This delicately flowing design of intertwined vines, tendrils, leaves and flowers is inspired by embroidery from the sixteenth and seventeenth centuries.

WHAT YOU NEED

Large pattern sheet A
Ivory queen silk, 20 cm × 45 cm (8" × 18")
Pale pink silk satin for background,
   20 cm × 20 cm (8" × 8")
Light-weight Shapewell (Permashape),
   20 cm × 45 cm (8" × 18")
Light-weight Pellon, 45 cm × 65 cm
   (18" × 26")
Cream felt, 25 cm x 40 cm (10" × 16")
26-gauge and 28-gauge beading wire

Finished size 36 cm × 60 cm (14" × 24")

Threads

Anchor Marlitt	Symbol
1 skein 1213 (pink)	**1**
1 skein 1212 (off white)	**2**

Colour Streams Silken Strands
1 skein rose blush   **3**

The Thread Gatherer Silk 'n Colors
1 skein strawflower (cream)   **4**
1 skein maidenhair fern (green)   **5**

Needle Necessities
French Wool Overdyed 88, Giverny
   (pink/cream/green)   **6**

Kaalund Yarns
1 skein Fine Mulberry Silk FS 21
   (dark pink)   **7**
1 skein Mulberry Silk S 549 (mid-pink)   **8**
1 skein Mulberry Silk S 130 (pale pink)   **9**

Rajmahal Art Silks
1 skein 742 (damask rose)   **10**

The Caron Collection
1 skein Waterlilies rosebush
   (pink/soft green)   **11**

Minnamurra Stranded Cotton

1 skein 300 (pale pink/pale green) **12**

Kaalund Yarns

1 skein Indulgence coral (pinks/cream) **13**

One 100 m (100 yds) reel YLI pink silk
    thread (to match background pink)

Beads

Delica satin, size 11	*Symbol*
6 g DBR 678 (mid-pink)	**1**
6 g DBR 672 (cream)	**2**
6 g DBR 828 (green)	**3**
3 g DBR satin mix	**9**

Other beads

6 g dark pink satin *	**4**
3 g two-cut pale pink, 2 mm	**5**
45 ivory pearls, size 1.5	**6**
1 ivory pearl, 5 mm	**7**
1 ivory pearl, 4 mm	**8**

STITCH SYMBOLS

A	stem stitch
AA	whipped stem stitch
B	chain stitch
BB	whipped chain stitch
C	French knot
D	granitos stitch (8 stitches)
E	laid stitch
F	detached chain stitch
G	close fly stitch
H	fly stitch
I	close long buttonhole stitch
II	close long and short buttonhole stitch
J	close short buttonhole stitch
K	long and short satin stitch
L	straight stitches
M	double knot stitch
N	cross stitch
P	feather stitch
Q	herringbone stitch

*   Size irregular — available from Bead Trimming and Craft.

METHOD

This design is composed of various embroidered and beaded shapes arranged on a quilted background with a twisted cord vine and covered wire tendrils. The patterns for the shapes are numbered and for each there is an actual-size pattern and an accompanying stitching diagram. The placement of the shapes on the vine is shown in sequence on pattern sheet A, starting at the top of the design and working in a clockwise direction. Two strands of thread are used for embroidery, unless otherwise marked on the stitching diagram.

Pattern 1

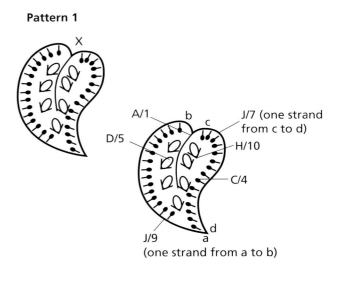

Pattern 2

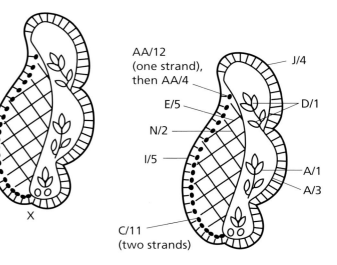

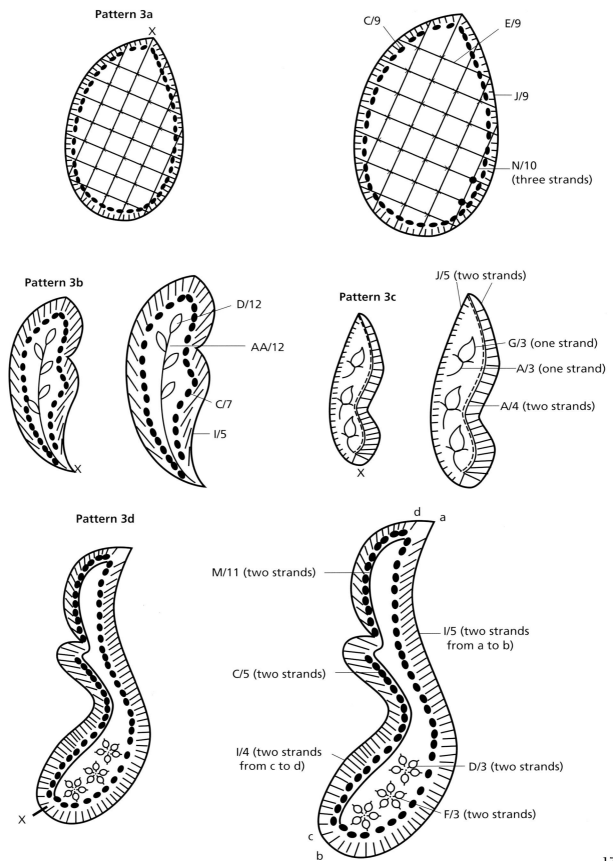

Pattern 3a

X

C/9   E/9

J/9

N/10
(three strands)

Pattern 3b

D/12

AA/12

C/7

I/5

X

Pattern 3c

J/5 (two strands)

G/3 (one strand)

A/3 (one strand)

A/4 (two strands)

X

Pattern 3d

d   a

M/11 (two strands)

I/5 (two strands
from a to b)

C/5 (two strands)

I/4 (two strands
from c to d)

D/3 (two strands)

F/3 (two strands)

X

c

b

17

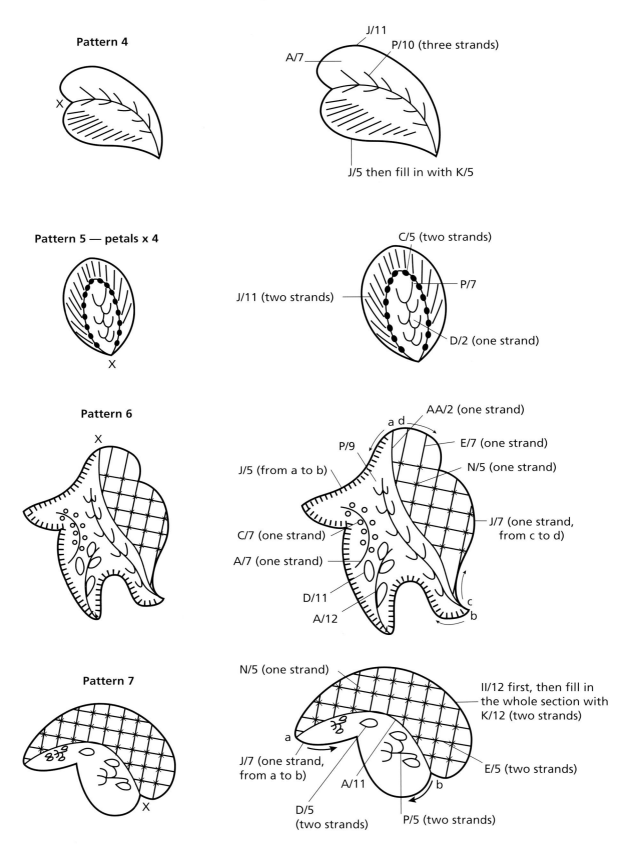

Pattern 4

J/11

P/10 (three strands)

A/7

J/5 then fill in with K/5

Pattern 5 — petals x 4

C/5 (two strands)

J/11 (two strands)

P/7

D/2 (one strand)

X

Pattern 6

X

AA/2 (one strand)

a d

P/9

E/7 (one strand)

J/5 (from a to b)

N/5 (one strand)

C/7 (one strand)

J/7 (one strand, from c to d)

A/7 (one strand)

D/11

c

A/12

b

Pattern 7

N/5 (one strand)

II/12 first, then fill in the whole section with K/12 (two strands)

a

J/7 (one strand, from a to b)

A/11

E/5 (two strands)

b

D/5 (two strands)

P/5 (two strands)

X

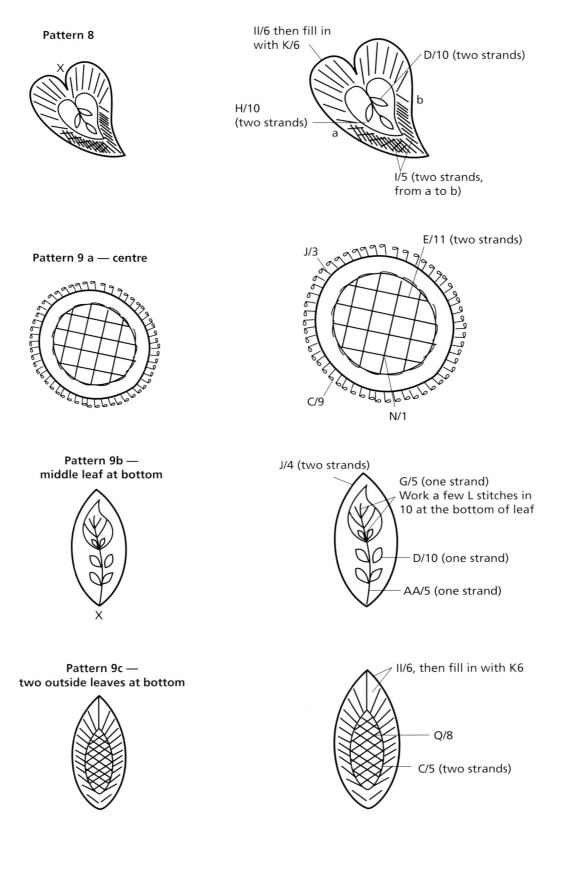

Pattern 8

X

II/6 then fill in
with K/6

D/10 (two strands)

b

H/10
(two strands)

a

I/5 (two strands,
from a to b)

Pattern 9 a — centre

E/11 (two strands)

J/3

C/9

N/1

**Pattern 9b —
middle leaf at bottom**

X

J/4 (two strands)

G/5 (one strand)
Work a few L stitches in
10 at the bottom of leaf

D/10 (one strand)

AA/5 (one strand)

**Pattern 9c —
two outside leaves at bottom**

II/6, then fill in with K6

Q/8

C/5 (two strands)

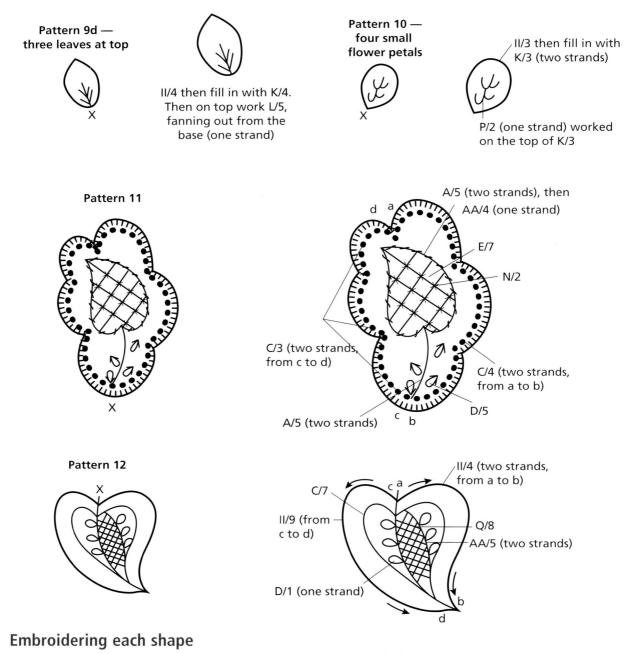

**Pattern 9d —
three leaves at top**

II/4 then fill in with K/4.
Then on top work L/5,
fanning out from the
base (one strand)

X

**Pattern 10 —
four small
flower petals**

II/3 then fill in with
K/3 (two strands)

X

P/2 (one strand) worked
on the top of K/3

Pattern 11

X

A/5 (two strands), then
AA/4 (one strand)

d a

E/7

N/2

C/3 (two strands,
from c to d)

C/4 (two strands,
from a to b)

A/5 (two strands)

c b

D/5

Pattern 12

X

C/7

II/9 (from
c to d)

II/4 (two strands,
from a to b)

c a

Q/8

AA/5 (two strands)

D/1 (one strand)

b

d

Embroidering each shape

1   Trace the pattern shape onto the silk fabric.

2   Place a piece of Shapewell underneath the silk and tack to hold.

3   Cut sufficient 28-gauge beading wire to go around the entire shape, crossing the wires slightly at point **X**.

4   Using stab stitches and two strands of pink silk thread matching the silk background fabric,

couch the wire onto the wrong side of the silk.

5   Turn the work over to the right side and embroider the shape following the stitch and thread symbols marked on the stitching diagram (for key to symbols, see *Stitch symbols* and *What you need*).

6   When the embroidery is finished, cut the shape out as close to the buttonholed edges as possible and trim off any excess wire.

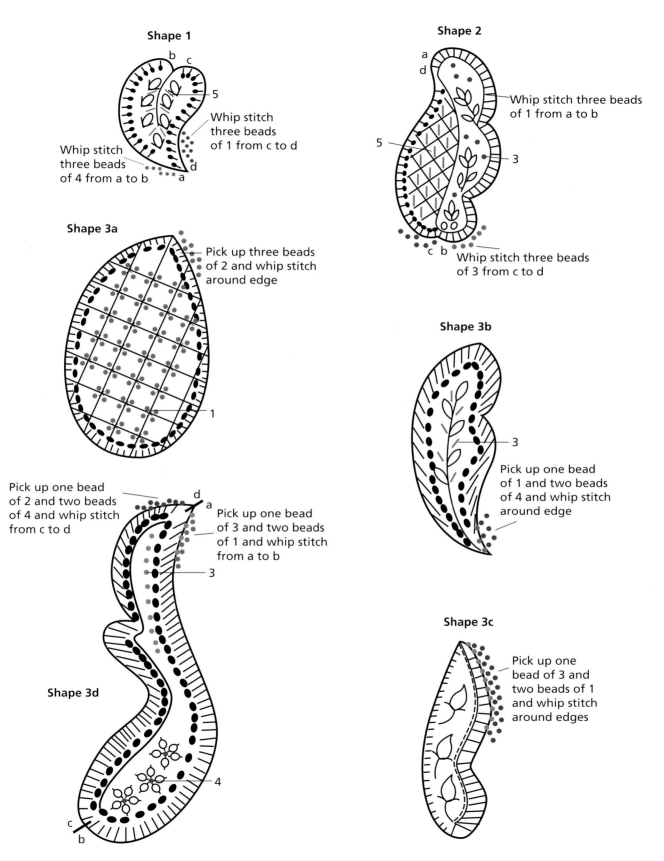

Shape 1

Whip stitch three beads of 1 from c to d

Whip stitch three beads of 4 from a to b

Shape 2

Whip stitch three beads of 1 from a to b

Whip stitch three beads of 3 from c to d

Shape 3a

Pick up three beads of 2 and whip stitch around edge

Shape 3b

Pick up one bead of 1 and two beads of 4 and whip stitch around edge

Pick up one bead of 2 and two beads of 4 and whip stitch from c to d

Pick up one bead of 3 and two beads of 1 and whip stitch from a to b

Shape 3d

Shape 3c

Pick up one bead of 3 and two beads of 1 and whip stitch around edges

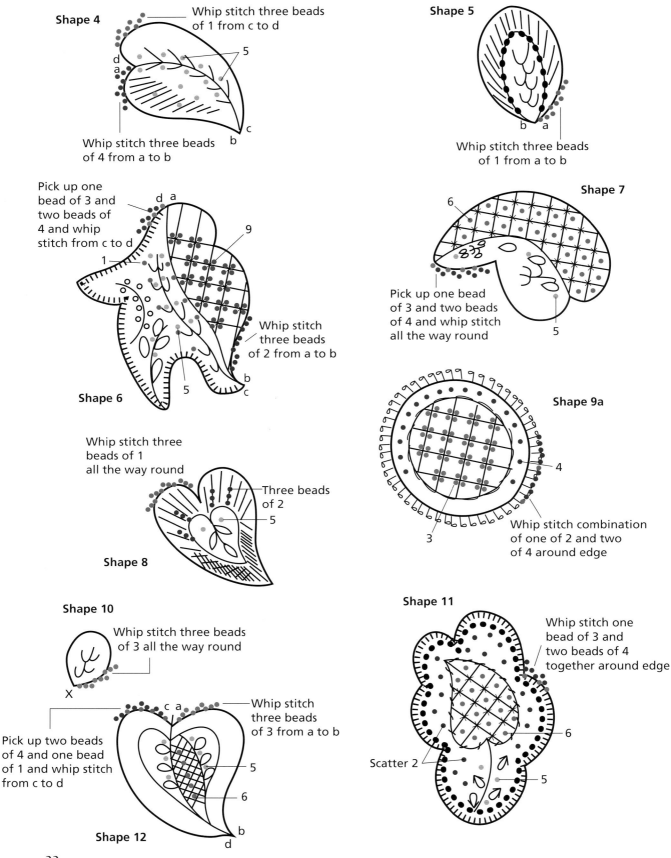

Shape 4

Whip stitch three beads
of 1 from c to d

Whip stitch three beads
of 4 from a to b

Shape 5

Whip stitch three beads
of 1 from a to b

Pick up one
bead of 3 and
two beads of
4 and whip
stitch from c to d

Whip stitch
three beads
of 2 from a to b

Shape 6

Shape 7

Pick up one bead
of 3 and two beads
of 4 and whip stitch
all the way round

Whip stitch three
beads of 1
all the way round

Three beads
of 2

Shape 8

Shape 9a

Whip stitch combination
of one of 2 and two
of 4 around edge

Shape 10

Whip stitch three beads
of 3 all the way round

X

Pick up two beads
of 4 and one bead
of 1 and whip stitch
from c to d

Whip stitch
three beads
of 3 from a to b

Shape 12

Shape 11

Whip stitch one
bead of 3 and
two beads of 4
together around edge

Scatter 2

Beading each shape

1   Cut a piece of 26-gauge wire the exact length of the shape (no excess wire is needed).

2   Place the wrong side of the shape on a piece of felt, sandwiching the cut wire in the centre between the embroidered shape and the felt. Tack in place.

3   Work the beading through all thicknesses, following the symbols in the beading diagram (see *What you need* for key to symbols).

4   Trim away the felt, leaving it slightly smaller than the silk piece.

5   Cut another piece of felt slightly larger than the silk and felt shape. Place the felt underneath the shape and pin or tack in place. Following the beading symbols for colours, pick up and whip stitch groups of three beads around the outside of each shape. Remove tacking stitches carefully.

To make the twisted vine

1   Trace the twisted vine pattern (see large pattern sheet A) onto the background silk fabric and mark a 1.5 cm (½") quilting grid all over.

2   Place the piece of Pellon under the silk and quilt the background fabric, using one strand of the fine pink silk thread.

3   Cut 3 m lengths of the following threads: one strand of **13**, two strands of **5**, all the strands of **2**. Fold in half and make a twisted cord.

4   Using one strand of **5**, stitch the twisted cord onto the vine design marked on the background silk by catching the cord at intervals to hold in place. Use an awl or a size 13 chenille needle to take the cord through to the wrong side of the fabric.

Attaching the shapes

Sew each shape in place onto the background fabric or the twisted cord with a few straight stitches at the top of each one. You may need to hold some shapes in place with a slip stitch underneath.

To make the twisted tendrils

1   Cut 14 lengths of 28-gauge wire, each roughly 13 cm (5") long. Follow steps 1–4 for each length of wire.

2   Using three strands of **5** and holding the thread over one end of the wire, fold the wire up and twist to hold thread. Holding the wire between your right thumb and finger and the thread in your left hand (or vice-versa if left-handed), continue to twist the wire so that the thread covers the wire.

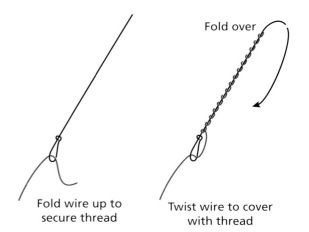

Fold over

Fold wire up to secure thread

Twist wire to cover with thread

3   When the wire is completely covered, fold it in half and twist the wires together tightly. If you prefer looser twists, wrap the wires around a satay stick or chopstick, and then remove the stick.

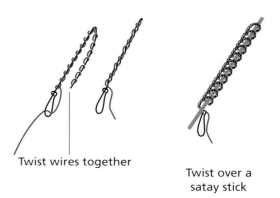

Twist wires together

Twist over a satay stick

4   With the length of thread still attached, sew the twisted covered wire tendrils into place along the corded vine. You should be able to slide part of each tendril underneath a section of the vine. Make sure the rough ends of the tendrils are hidden under the vine or a shape on the vine.

Jewellery box

This stunning bow in rich colours is a fitting adornment for the lid of a jewellery box.

WHAT YOU NEED

Black satin jewellery box, 17.5 cm × 10.5 cm × 6.5 cm (7" × 4¼" × 2½") (available from Rajmahal)

Black silk satin, 20 cm x 30 cm (8" × 12")

Green dupion silk shot with bright pink, 20 cm × 30 cm (8" × 12")

Light-weight Shapewell (Permashape), 20 cm × 30 cm (8" × 12")

Thick Vilene, one piece 20 cm × 45 cm (8" × 20") and one piece 20 cm x 20 cm (8" × 8")

Soluweb, 20 cm x 20 cm (8" × 8")

Black felt, 20 cm x 30 cm (8" × 12")

11 mm (¾") self-cover button

24-gauge, 26-gauge and 28-gauge beading wire

Size of box lid 17.5 cm × 10.5 cm (7" × 4¼")

Threads

The Thread Gatherer Silk 'n Colors **Symbol**

1 skein 39 (mauveberry) **1**

Anchor Marlitt

1 skein 1029 (yellow-green) **2**

1 skein 815 (fuschia) **3**

1 skein 801 (black) **AM 801**

Anchor Reflecta metallic

1 reel (100 m/110 yds) 313 (green) **4**

1 reel (100 m/110 yds) 311 (pink) **5**

Anchor Stranded Cotton

2 skeins 255 (green) **6**

Cascade House Australia

1 skein Stranded Silk 3345 (pink) **7**

Beads

Delica, size 11

6 g DBR 10 (black)

3 g DBR 902 (pink)

5 g DBR 508 (pink/green)

Bugle beads

3 g bright green, 2 mm

6 g two-cut black, approx. 2 mm

Crystals

32 vitrail crystal flowers, 4 mm

18 fuschia crystal bicones, 4 mm

2 fuschia round faceted crystals, 6 mm

STITCH SYMBOLS

A   stem stitch

AA   whipped stem stitch

BB   whipped chain stitch

E   laid stitch

F   close fly stitch

FF   granitos stitch

G   detached chain stitch

H   close fly stitch

I   close long buttonhole stitch

J   long and short satin stitch

K   straight stitches

L   cross stitch

M   French knot

METHOD

Embroidering the bow

Use one strand of thread unless instructed otherwise.

1   Trace the two half-bow designs onto the soluweb, marking only the main lines and flipping the design so that the second half-bow is a mirror image of the first.

2   Working one half of the bow at a time, tack soluweb onto the right side of the black silk.

3   Using one strand of **AM 801**, work a row of small tacking stitches around the outline of the half-bow.

4   Work the embroidery following the stitching diagram and thread and stitch symbols. Then turn the work to the wrong side.

Half-bow pattern and stitching diagram

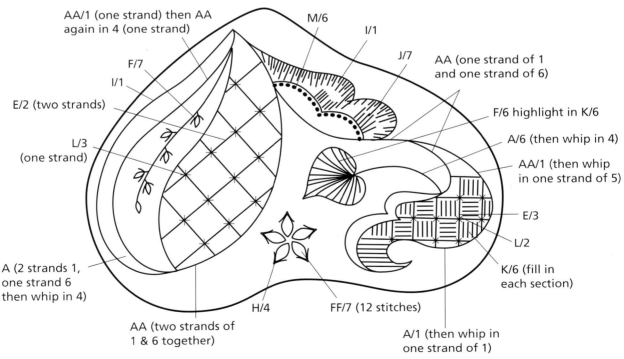

AA/1 (one strand) then AA again in 4 (one strand)

M/6

I/1

F/7

J/7

I/1

AA (one strand of 1 and one strand of 6)

E/2 (two strands)

F/6 highlight in K/6

L/3 (one strand)

A/6 (then whip in 4)

AA/1 (then whip in one strand of 5)

E/3

L/2

A (2 strands 1, one strand 6 then whip in 4)

K/6 (fill in each section)

H/4

FF/7 (12 stitches)

AA (two strands of 1 & 6 together)

A/1 (then whip in one strand of 1)

5   Cut a length of 26-gauge wire to fit all around the half-bow shape, overlapping the wire slightly at **X**, as shown in wiring diagram.

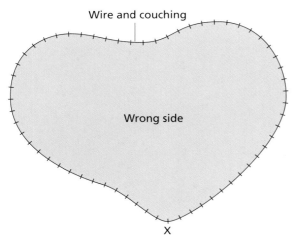

6   Using two strands of **AM 801** and stab stitches, and following the tacking line, couch the wire onto the wrong side of the half-bow.

7   Turn the work to the right side and, starting at **X**, use two strands of **AM 801** to work close short buttonhole stitch over the wire, as shown.

8   Cut the half-bow shape out as close to the buttonholed edge as possible and cut off excess wire.

9   Dissolve the soluweb (see *Materials*).

10   Cut a length of wire to fit the half-bow and bend as shown below.

11   Place the wrong side of the half-bow onto a larger piece of felt, sandwiching the wire between the bow and the felt, and tack in place through all thicknesses.

Beading the bow

1.   Work the beading through all thicknesses, following the beading symbols.

2   Cut away the felt around the half-bow shape so that it is slightly smaller than the piece of silk and remove tacking stitches carefully.

3   Place the half-bow, right side up, on another piece of black felt that is slightly larger than the beaded shape, and pin in place.

4   Pick up one of **10**, one of **9** and one of **10**, and whip stitch groups of this combination all around the outside of the half-bow shape.

5   Bead second half-bow shape in the same way.

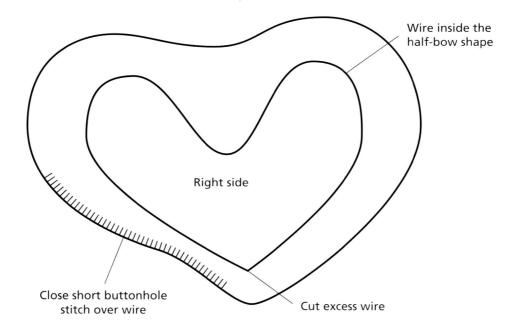

Beading guide

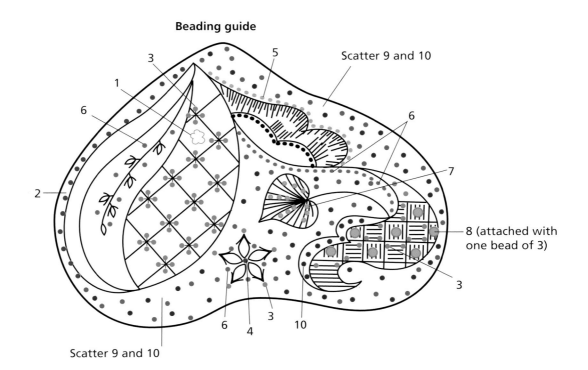

3

1

6

2

5

Scatter 9 and 10

6

7

6

8 (attached with one bead of 3)

3

6   4   3   10

Scatter 9 and 10

Key to beading symbols

1   Vitrail crystal flower secured with DBR 508

2   Combination of DBR 508/902/508

3   One DBR 508 bead

4   One 6 mm fuschia round crystal

5   Pick up three of DBR 902

6   2 mm green bugle bead

7   Pick up three of DBR 508

8   4 mm fuschia crystal bicone

9   2 mm two-cut black

10   DBR 10

Making the leaves

Follow these instructions for each of the 15 leaves.

1   Trace the leaf pattern onto Vilene.

2   Cut a length of 28-gauge wire to fit around the leaf shape, overlapping the ends slightly at **X**. Couch wire in place using two strands of **6**.

3   Turn the work over and, using two strands of **6**, work long and short buttonhole stitch around the outside of the leaf.

4   Fill in the rest of the leaf with long and short satin stitch, keeping the stitches in one direction as shown.

5   Using one strand of **2**, work a few straight stitches on the top of the leaf, fanning out from **X**. Repeat with one strand of **4**.

6   Carefully cut the leaf out as close to the edge of the buttonhole stitching as possible.

7   Whip stitch one bead of **10** closely all around the edge of the leaf.

Highlight first
with 2 then 4

Leaf beading

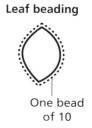

One bead
of 10

Making the centre flower

1   Cut a piece of light-weight Pellon to fit the self-cover button. Place the Pellon on top of the button and then cover the button following the instructions with the button.

2   Attach nine leaves around the outside with a few stitches, then attach another row of seven leaves inside the first row.

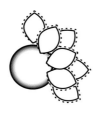

3   For the centre of the button, I have used a piece of jewellery in the shape of a flower. Alternatively, you could fill the centre with more crystals or work more leaves in the pink silk (**7**) and sew a large crystal in the centre.

Assembling the bow and attaching to box

1   Place right sides of the half-bows together, overstitch at point **X** and open out.

2   Sew the button flower to the centre of the bow.

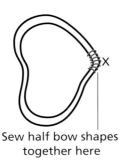

Sew half bow shapes
together here

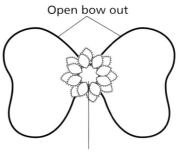

Open bow out

Sew button in place

3   Remove the padded insert from the lid of the jewellery box and cover it in the green silk, following the instructions with the box.

4   Replace (do not glue) the covered lid insert in the lid. Pick up one of **10**, one of **3** and one of **10** beads, and whip stitch this combination around the edge of the lid, catching the black satin edge of the lid and the green silk. Repeat all around the edge of the lid.

5   Using a beading needle and beading thread, sew the centre of the bow to the lid of the jewellery box with a few straight stitches. Bend the bow into shape.

Hippeastrum

This delightful flower will add a touch of elegance to any head wear, no matter what the season or occasion.

WHAT YOU NEED

Vilene, 20 cm × 20 cm (8" × 8")
Soluweb, 15 cm × 15 cm (6" × 6")
Green felt, 2.5 cm × 1.5 cm (1" × ¾")
3 g Delica satin beads 672 (cream), size 11
28-gauge beading wire
Six stamens, one of which should be larger
    and slightly different from the others
    (available from cake decoration suppliers)
Double-sided adhesive tape

Finished size 13 cm × 13 cm (5"× 5")

Threads

Kaalund Yarns Fine Wool (FW)

4 skeins 2400 (natural)
2 skeins 2437 (pale pink)
1 skein 2436 (mid-pink)
1 skein 2472 (green)

Kaalund Yarns Fine Mulberry Silk (FS)

1 skein FS 3 (pale pink)
1 skein FS 130 (pink)
1 skein FS 5 (mid-pink)
1 skein FS 104 (dark pink)
2 skeins FS 45 (natural)

Anchor Stranded Cotton (ASC)

1 skein of 301 (pale yellow)
1 skein of 2 (natural)
1 skein of 257 (green)

METHOD

The flower has six petals: an identical pair, embroidered in the same way; a second pair with one worked in reverse; one back petal and one front petal. Use one strand of thread for embroidery unless stated otherwise.

Pair of identical petals

1   Trace the petal pattern below onto Vilene.

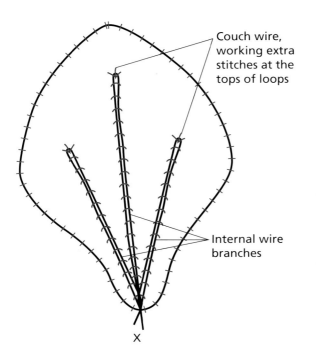

Couch wire, working extra stitches at the tops of loops

Internal wire branches

X

2   Cut a length of wire to fit all the way round the petal shape, overlapping the wires slightly at **X**. Couch in place using two strands of **FW 2400.**

3   Measure and cut three pieces of wire double the length of each of the three internal branches. Fold each piece in half. Using two strands of **FW 2400**, couch the centre branch in place. Then fold the right-hand branch and couch in place, followed by the left-hand branch. Work extra stitches at the top of the wire loops to hold securely.

4   Turn the work over and, using **FW 2400**, embroider long and short buttonhole stitch around the edge of the petal. Fill the remainder of the petal in with long and short satin stitch in **FW 2400**, following the stitch direction shown below.

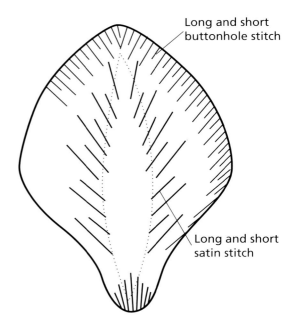

Long and short buttonhole stitch

Long and short satin stitch

5   Using two strands of **FW 2400**, work two rows of chain stitch close together up the centre of the petal. Work some more long and short satin stitches in **FW 2400** over the chain stitch to blend with the other stitching. This creates a raised effect to define the central vein of the petal. (See diagrams a and b.)

6   Work some more long and short satin stitches in **FW 2437** on top of the **FW 2400** satin stitching up to the pattern lines marked on either side of the raised centre vein.

7   Work a few straight stitches in **FW 2436** from the marked lines to the edge of the petal.

8   Using matching threads (i.e. **FS 45** with **FW 2400** and **FS 130** with **FW 2437**), highlight the petals with straight stitches in silk on top of the wool, blending the colours.

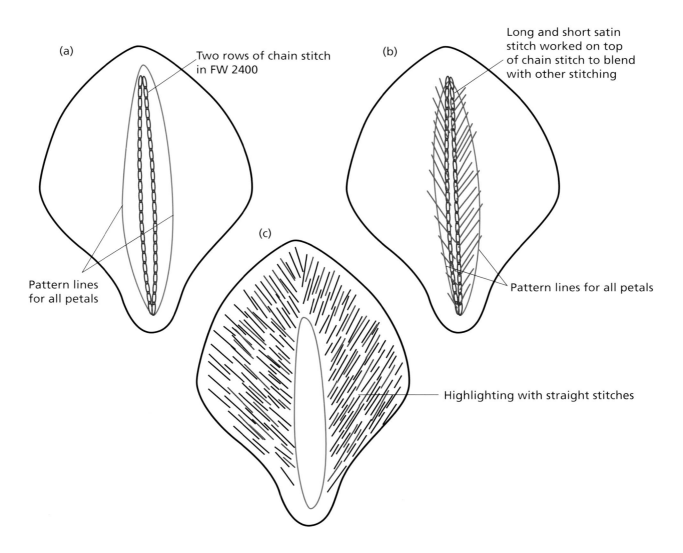

(a)

Two rows of chain stitch in FW 2400

Pattern lines for all petals

(b)

Long and short satin stitch worked on top of chain stitch to blend with other stitching

Pattern lines for all petals

(c)

Highlighting with straight stitches

9 Fanning out from the centre as shown in diagram c, embroider a few long straight stitches using **FS 104**.

10 Continue with instructions for all petals, steps 1–4 (see below).

Second pair of petals (one worked in reverse)

Work steps 1–6 as for the identical pair of petals.

7 Referring to the diagram on page 36 and using **FW 2436**, work straight stitches on side AA of the petal on one side of markings, then highlight with **FS 5**. Highlight this side of the

petal with more straight stitches in matching silk thread **FS 104**.

8 Referring to the diagram on page 36, highlight side BB with straight stitches in **FW 2437**, and then highlight this side with more straight stitches in **FS 45**. Scatter a few pale pink straight stitches in **FW 2437**, and then highlight on top of the wool with **FS 3**.

9 Fanning out from the centre, embroider a few long straight stitches using **FS 104**.

10 Continue with instructions for all petals, steps 1–4.

Second pair of petals

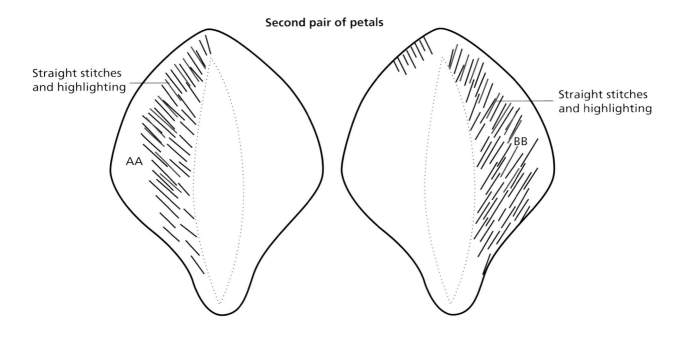

Straight stitches and highlighting

Straight stitches and highlighting

AA

BB

Back petal

Work steps 1–5 as for identical pair of petals.

6   Using **FW 2436** work long and short satin stitches on top of the **FW 2400**. Then highlight on top of the **FW 2436** with **FS 5** and on top of **FW 2400** with **FS 45**.

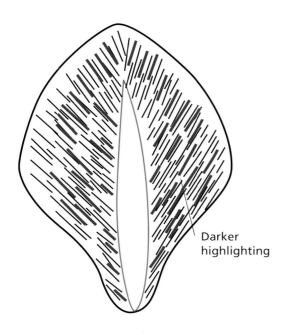

Darker highlighting

7   Fanning out from the centre , embroider a few long straight stitches using **FS 104**.

8   Continue with instructions for all petals, steps 1–4.

Front petal

Work steps 1–5 as for identical pair of petals, following the diagrams opposite for pattern, wiring and stitch direction.

6   Highlight the entire petal with straight stitches in **FS 45**. Using **FS 5**, work a few long straight stitches at the tip of the petal.

7   Fanning out from the centre, embroider a few long straight stitches using **FS 104**.

8   Continue with instructions for all petals, steps 1–2.

9   Attach rows of Delica 672 beads fanning out from the centre in varying lengths, as illustrated on the diagram showing sequence for attaching petals (see page 39).

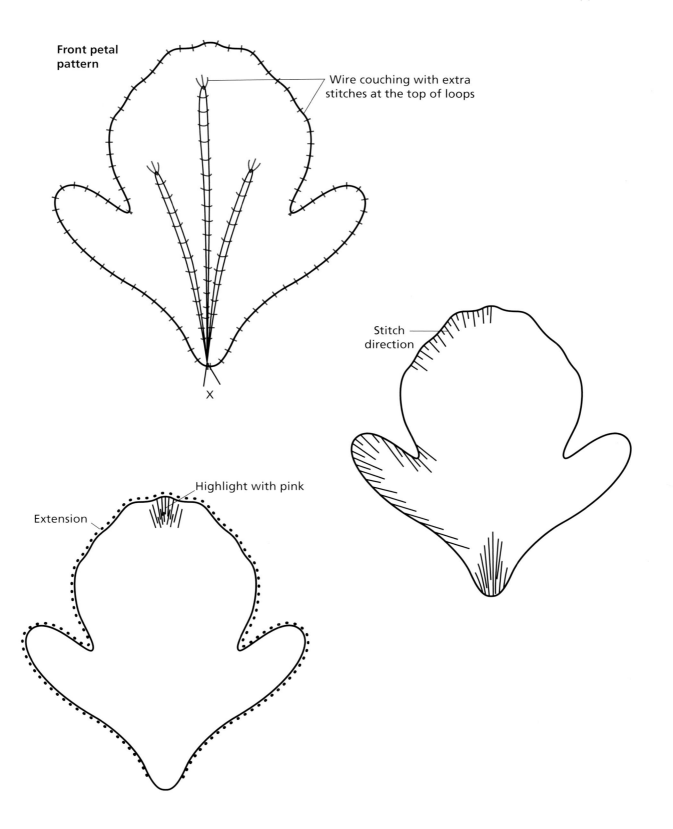

Front petal pattern

Wire couching with extra stitches at the top of loops

X

Stitch direction

Highlight with pink

Extension

All petals

1   Using **FW 2472**, embroider a few straight stitches at the base of each petal. Then embroider a few straight stitches on top of the wool with one strand of **ASC 301**.

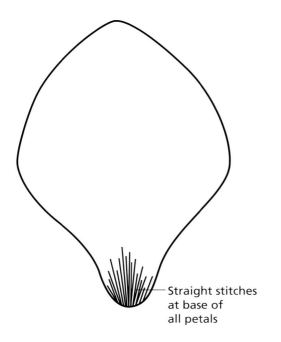

Straight stitches at base of all petals

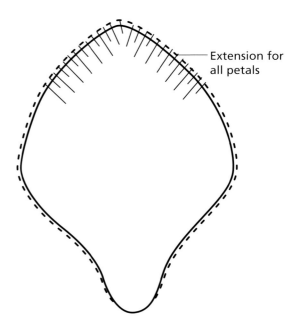

Extension for all petals

2   Carefully cut the petal out close to the buttonhole stitches and cut off any excess wire.

3   Place the petal right side up on top of a piece of soluweb and pin in place. With **FW 2400** embroider an extension row of close long and short buttonhole stitches as shown in the diagram. Using **FS 45**, work another row on top of the wool using slightly more open long and short buttonhole stitches.

4   Dissolve the soluweb (see *Materials* for method).

Assembling the flower

1   Using five identical stamens and one slightly larger, different-shaped stamen , cut a piece of double-sided adhesive tape and place the base of the stamens close together on the tape. Roll the tape tightly round the base of the stamens. Peel off the backing paper, cut a short strip of green felt and wrap around the tape once, overlapping slightly.

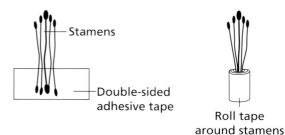

Stamens

Double-sided adhesive tape

Roll tape around stamens

2   Using two strands of **ASC 257** and following the sequence shown in the diagram, attach each petal to the green felt wrapped around the stamens, sewing close to the top of the felt and bending the bottom of each petal slightly as you sew.

3   Attach the flower to a hat piece.

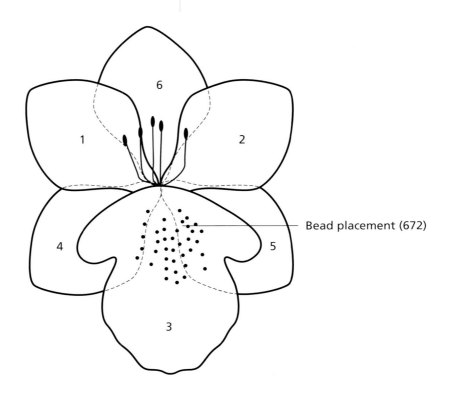

Bead placement (672)

Large leaf pattern and wiring diagram

Large leaf stitch direction

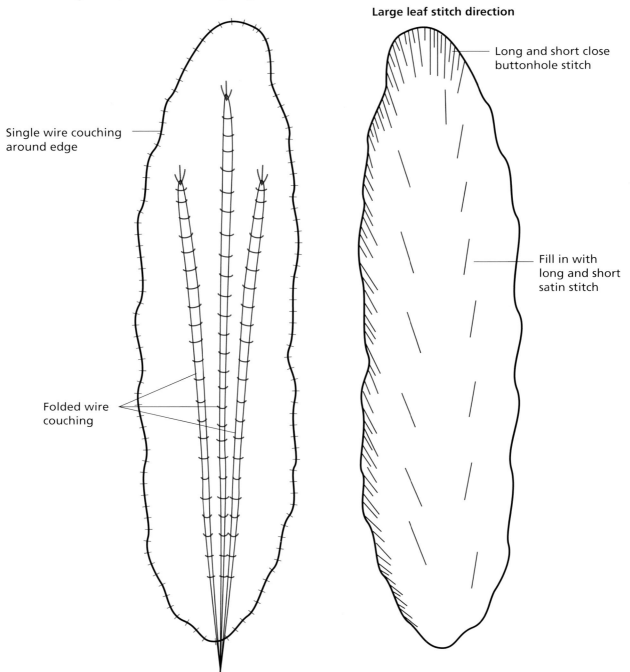

Single wire couching around edge

Long and short close buttonhole stitch

Fill in with long and short satin stitch

Folded wire couching

MAKE A PICTURE

Instead of using the flower as the focal point of a hat piece, you could make it into a picture with a stem and two leaves. You will need an additional four skeins of **FW 2472**, extra Vilene and soluweb, background fabric of your choice and a 30 cm (12") length of very thin dowel.

Large leaf

1   Trace the large leaf pattern onto Vilene. Cut wire and couch around the edge following the method used for the petals.

2   Cut a piece of wire double the length of each vein. Fold the wire in half and, starting with the centre vein, couch the wire in place working extra stitches at the top. Repeat for the other two veins.

3   Turn the work over and, using **FW 2472**, work close long and short buttonhole stitch around the edge of the leaf over the wire. Fill in the leaf with long and short satin stitch in the same thread.

4   Carefully cut the leaf out close to the buttonhole stitching. Place it right side up onto a piece of soluweb and pin in place. Work an extension row of close long and short buttonhole stitch from the soluweb onto the previous buttonhole stitching.

5   Dissolve the soluweb.

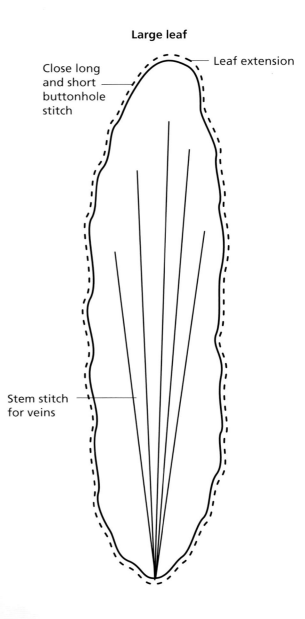

Large leaf

Leaf extension

Close long and short buttonhole stitch

Stem stitch for veins

Small leaf

1   Trace the small leaf pattern onto Vilene. Cut wire and couch around the edge following the method used for the petals.

2   Continue with steps 2–5 as for the large leaf.

Stem

1   Trace the stem pattern onto Vilene, extending the length to 30 cm (12").

2   Using **FW 2472**, work a row of close short buttonhole stitch around the outside and then fill the stem with long and short satin stitch.

3   Place the wrong side of the stem on top of a piece of soluweb and work an extension row of close long and short buttonhole stitch in **FW 2472**.

4   Dissolve the soluweb.

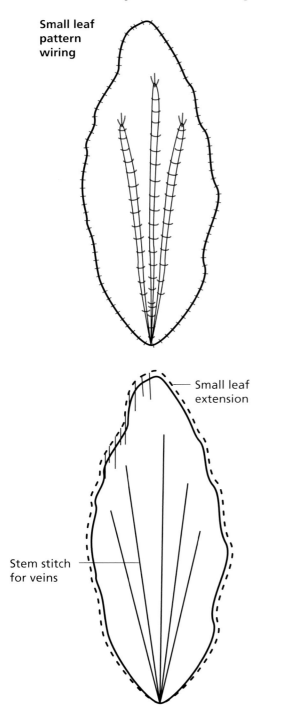

Small leaf pattern wiring

Small leaf extension

Stem stitch for veins

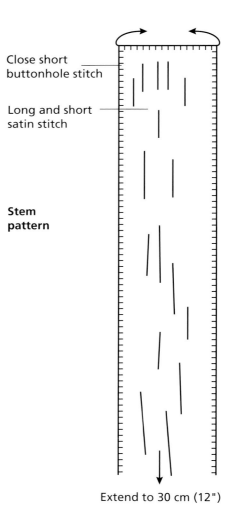

Close short buttonhole stitch

Long and short satin stitch

Stem pattern

Extend to 30 cm (12")

5 Cut the stem out and wrap around a very thin piece of dowel 30 cm (12") long.

Assembling the picture

1 Attach the stem to a background fabric with slip stitches down each side.

2 Place the smaller leaf on top of the larger leaf and sew them to the picture at the bottom of the stem.

3 Sew the flower head in place.

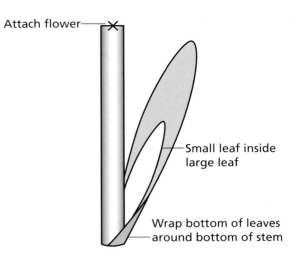

Attach flower — ✕

Small leaf inside large leaf

Wrap bottom of leaves around bottom of stem

Sapphire evening bag

This dazzling and colourful design worked on a black evening bag adds just the right touch for a special night out. Embroider the flower on its own for a brooch or a shoe ornament.

WHAT YOU NEED

A piece of dark blue or aqua silk, approx. 4 cm × 4 cm (1½" × 1½")

Medium or thick Vilene, 20 cm × 115 cm (8" × 45")

3 pieces felt, each 20 cm × 20 cm (8" × 8")

24-gauge and 26-gauge beading wire

15 mm self-cover button

Small piece of Pellon to fit the top of the button

Threads

One skein of each of the following:

Kaalund Yarns	Symbol
2-ply Wool 2259 (light aqua)	**1**
Fine Wool 2410 (medium mauve)	**2**
Woollie 2-ply, sapphire	**3**
Skink, sapphire	**4**
Ambrosia, sapphire	**5**
Wispers, sapphire	**6**
Indulgence, sapphire	**6**

Rajmahal Art Silk	
786 (blue heaven)	**7**

Colour Streams	
Exotic Lights 21 (purple genie)	**8**

Anchor	
Marlitt 859 (purple)	**9**
Stranded Cotton 1066 (dark aqua)	**ASC 1066**

Beads

Delica, size 11	Symbol
6 g DBR 694 (mauve)	**1**
6 g DBR 626 (aqua)	**2**
6 g DBR 63 (bright blue)	**3**
3 g DBR 880 (mid-blue)	**4**
3 g DBR 502 (silver multi-coloured)	**5**
3 g DBR 914 (bright pink)	**6**

Other beads	
30 dark sapphire blue bicones, 4 mm	**7**
10 light amethyst crystal flowers, 5 mm	**8**
1 royal blue cut (faceted) glass bead, 4 mm	**9**
Czech jade lustre cut glass beads, 5 mm, to bead the edge of the handbag	

STITCH SYMBOLS

A   stem stitch

AA   whipped stem stitch

B   detached chain stitch

C   granitos stitch

D   laid stitch

E   cross stitch

F   straight stitch

G   feather stitch

H   close long and short buttonhole stitch

I   long and short satin stitch

J   couching

K   French knot

L   close short buttonhole stitch

METHOD

Stitch and thread symbols are used for the embroidery that is worked on top of the base embroidery: e.g. A represents stem stitch. 2 represents Kaalund Yarns Fine Wool 2410, so A/1 means work stem stitch in Kaalund Yarns Fine Wool 2410.

All shapes

Follow these steps for leaves A–E and the flower petals.

1   Trace each shape onto Vilene and place the work in an embroidery hoop.

2   Cut a length of wire to fit around the shape, leaving a small tail at the bottom.

3   Using two strands of **ASC 1066** and starting at **X**, couch the wire around the shapes. This is the wrong side of the work.

Arrangement of shapes for front of evening bag.

You may need to vary this arrangement slightly to suit the shape of the evening bag used.

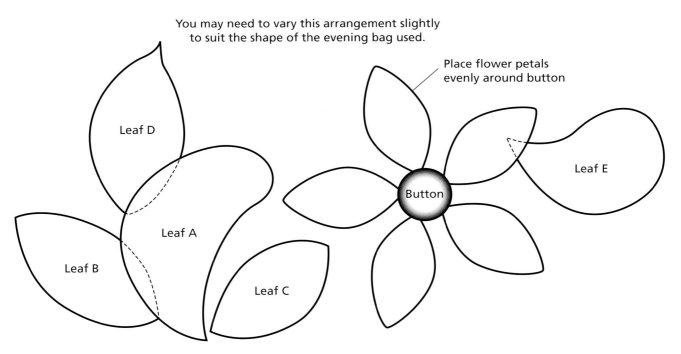

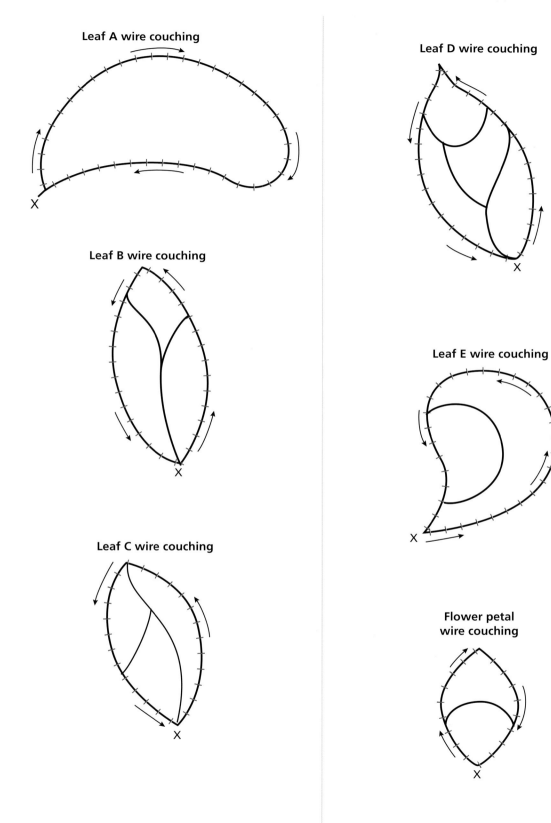

Leaf A wire couching

Leaf D wire couching

Leaf B wire couching

Leaf C wire couching

Leaf E wire couching

**Flower petal
wire couching**

4   Turn the work over and place it back in the hoop.

5   On the right side, work long and short buttonhole stitch over the wire in the colours indicated in the base embroidery diagrams. Some areas are worked in close short buttonhole stitch, and then long and short satin stitches are worked up to the edge of the buttonhole stitch. Fill in the shapes as shown in long and short satin stitch, keeping the stitches going in the same direction.

Leaf B base embroidery: stitch direction and colours

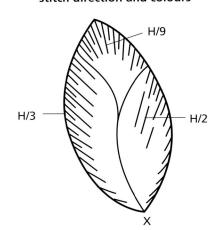

Leaf A base embroidery: stitch direction and colours

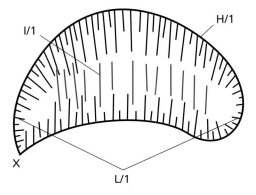
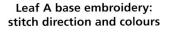

Leaf B top embroidery

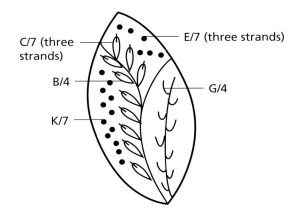

Leaf A top embroidery

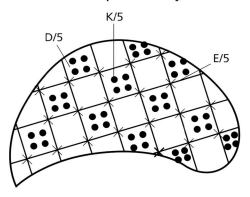

Leaf C base embroidery: stitch direction and colours

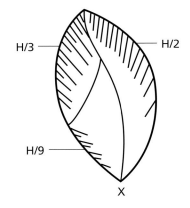

Leaf C top embroidery

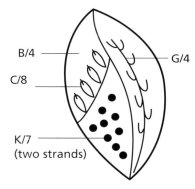

B/4

C/8

G/4

K/7
(two strands)

Leaf E base embroidery: stitch direction and colours

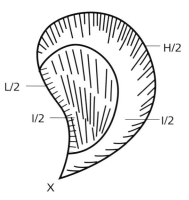

H/2

L/2

I/2

I/2

X

Leaf D base embroidery: stitch direction and colours

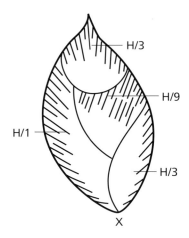

H/3

H/9

H/1

H/3

X

Leaf E top embroidery

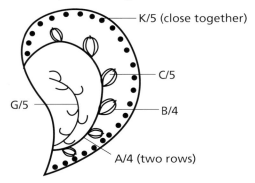

K/5 (close together)

C/5

G/5

B/4

A/4 (two rows)

Flower petals base embroidery: stitch direction and colour

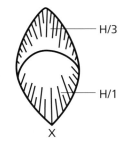

H/3

H/1

X

Leaf D top embroidery

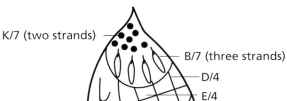

K/7 (two strands)

B/7 (three strands)

D/4

E/4

G/4

Flower petals top embroidery

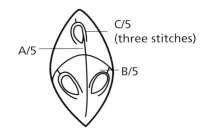

C/5
(three stitches)

A/5

B/5

Internal wiring for leaf and petal shapes

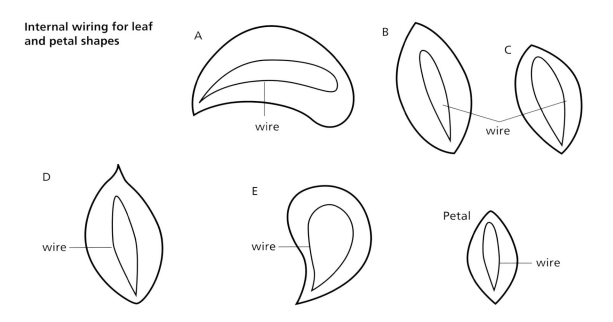

6 Work the top embroidery over the base embroidery following the symbols in the diagrams (for key to symbols, see *Stitch symbols* and *What you need*).

7 When all the embroidery is complete, carefully cut out each shape as close as possible to the buttonholed edge and trim excess wire.

8 For each shape, cut a length of 24-gauge wire as shown in the internal wiring diagrams. Sandwich the wire between the embroidered design and a piece of felt, and tack together. Work on only a couple of shapes at a time in your hoop.

Leaf A beading

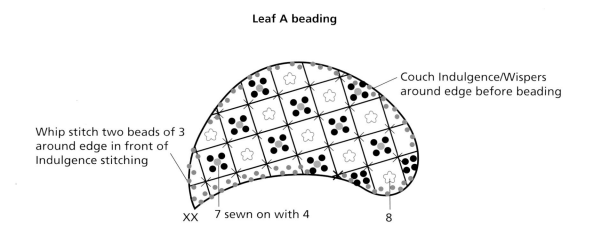

9   Work the beading for each shape through all thicknesses, following the symbols in the beading diagrams (for key to symbols, see *What you need*).

Leaf B beading

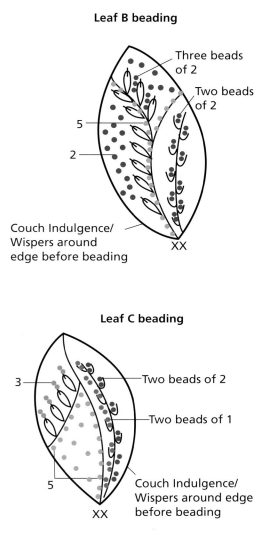

Three beads of 2

Two beads of 2

5

2

Couch Indulgence/ Wispers around edge before beading

XX

Leaf C beading

3

Two beads of 2

Two beads of 1

5

Couch Indulgence/ Wispers around edge before beading

XX

Leaf D beading

Couch Indulgence/ Wispers around edge before beading

5

Two beads of 1

4

2

5

Two beads of 4

Two beads of 3

Three beads of 1

XX

Leaf E beading

Two beads of 5

Fill in area with 4

Fill in with 1

Couch Indulgence/ Wispers around edge before beading

XX

Whip stitch three beads of 2 around edge of shape

Flower petals beading

7 sewn on with one bead of 5

Three beads of 5

3

2

Two beads of 1

6

XX

Whip stitch combination of six Delica beads, alternating beads 1 and 3, around edge

10 Cut away the felt slightly smaller than the embroidered shape and remove tacking.

11 Place each shape onto another piece of felt and tack in place. Trim the felt away leaving it slightly larger than the embroidered shape.

12 Twist together two strands of Indulgence or Wispers thread (**6**) and, starting at **XX** couch in place around the edges of each shape with one strand of **3** or beading thread, catching the felt and the buttonholed edges as you go.

13 Whip stitch beads around the edges of the shapes over the Indulgence/Wispers or just inside the shape, as indicated on the beading diagrams.

Beading the button

1 Cut a piece of Pellon the size of the top of the button. Cover the button in dark blue or acqua silk following the self-cover directions. Before pulling the thread up, place the piece of Pellon between the button and the silk, then pull the thread up and secure. Assemble the button.

2 Using double beading thread, secure it in the centre of the button. Pick up the royal blue cut glass bead (**9**) and one bead of **3**, take the needle back down through the cut glass bead and secure in place.

3 Sew six bicones (**7**) around the cut glass bead, attaching these with one bead of **2**.

4 Bring the needle close to the bicones and pick up a combination of five Delica beads (mixed colours of your choice). Take the needle out to the edge of the button and repeat all the way round.

5 Pick up another combination of three Delica beads, starting with a bright pink (**6**), and whip stitch around the edge of the button.

Assembling the flower

1 Place a piece of Vilene in the hoop. Sew each petal onto the Vilene to form the flower, leaving a small space in the centre for the button.

2 Sew the beaded button in the centre.

3 Trim away the excess Vilene from around the flower shape, leaving a small amount on the back to attach to the bag.

Attaching the shapes to the bag

1 Sew leaf shapes B and D to the back leaf A, so that they fan out behind it.

2 Using a beading needle and beading thread, secure the flower, leaf group ABD and other leaves to the evening bag with a few stitches.

3 Whip stitch Czech cut glass beads around the edge of the flap.

Cream delight

In this delicate design of leaves, flowers, berries, acorns and butterflies, a variety of threads in one colour and tone are used to create different textures and effects.

WHAT YOU NEED

Chocolate brown dupion silk for background, 60 cm × 115/90 cm (24" × 45/36")

Medium or thick Vilene, 60 cm × 115 cm (24" × 45")

Shapewell (Permashape), 60 cm × 115 cm (24" × 45")

1 square of beige felt, 20 cm x 20 cm (8" × 8")

Soluweb, 20 cm × 90 cm (8" × 36")

1 bunch very fine stamens

26-gauge and 28-gauge beading wire

Finished size of design 17 cm × 17 cm (6½" × 6½")

Threads

Kaalund Yarns Fine Wool (FW)
2 skeins 2400 (natural)
1 skein 2423 (light beige)

Kaalund Yarns Fine Mulberry Silk (FS)
1 skein FS 45 (natural)

Kaalund Yarns 2-ply Wool (KW)
1 skein 3100 (natural)

Anchor Stranded Cotton (ASC)
1 skein each 904 (light brown), 926 (light beige), 388 (beige), 367 (tan), 380 (brown)
2 skeins 275 (cream)

Anchor Marlitt (AM)
1 skein 872 (deep beige)
1 skein 1036 (beige)

Anchor Lamé (AL)
1 skein 303 (gold)

YLI Silk Floss (YLI)
1 packet 000 (off white)

Rajmahal Art Silk (RAS)
1 skein ecru

Cascade House Stranded Silk (CH)
1 card 1000 (natural)
1 card 2355 (beige)

Beads

Mill Hill (MH)

1 packet cream pebble beads

3 packets petite glass seed beads 40123 (cream)

2 packets 2.5 mm seed beads 00123 (cream)

Other beads

6g Delica DBC 22 (bronze), size 11

4 bronze two-cut beads, 2 mm

2 cream pearls, size 1.5

3 pony beads, 9 mm

METHOD

The picture is composed of leaves intermingled with three flowers, a blossom, some berries and acorns, and two butterflies. Unless stated otherwise, 28-gauge beading wire is used, all the wire couching is done on the wrong side of the work and all embroidery is done with one strand.

Leaf A (work two)

1 Trace the pattern onto Vilene.

2 Cut a length of wire to fit around the leaf shape.

3 Using two strands of **ASC 275**, couch the wire in place, overlapping the wires slightly at **X**.

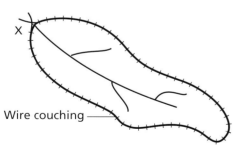

Wire couching

4 Turn work over. Using two strands of **ASC 275**, work close short buttonhole stitch over the wire.

5 Using one strand of **ASC 926**, work stem stitch along the centre vein and other veins.

6 Using one strand of **KW 3100** and one strand

of **RAS** ecru together, fill in the leaf between the veins and work French knots close to the buttonholed edge.

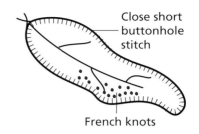

Close short buttonhole stitch

French knots

7 Carefully cut the leaf out close to the buttonholed edge and trim excess wire.

Leaf B (work two)

1 Trace the pattern onto Vilene.

2 Cut three pieces of wire double the length of the central vein and two branches, as shown in the diagram.

3 Fold each piece in half. Using two strands of **ASC 275**, couch the folded wire in place along the veins, starting with the centre vein and working extra stitches at the top of each loop.

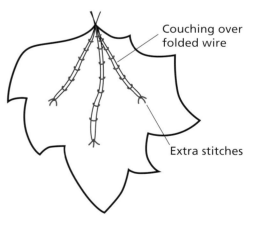

Couching over folded wire

Extra stitches

4 Turn the work over and using **FW 2400**, work close long and short buttonhole stitch all around the leaf.

5 Using **FW 2400**, fill in the rest of the leaf with long and short satin stitch.

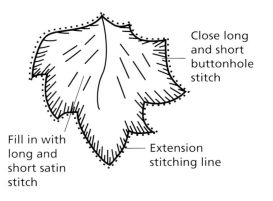

Close long and short buttonhole stitch

Fill in with long and short satin stitch

Extension stitching line

6   Carefully cut the leaf out close to the buttonholed edge and trim excess wire.

7   Repeat steps 1–6 to make the second leaf.

8   Place the two leaves on a piece of soluweb and pin to hold in place.

9   Use one strand of **RAS ecru** to work an extension row of close long and short buttonhole stitch all around each leaf.

10   Work stem stitch along the centre vein and branches using one strand of **AM 1036** on one leaf and one strand of **AM 872** on the other.

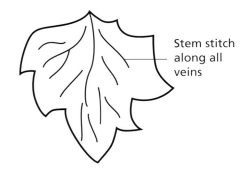

Stem stitch along all veins

11   Dissolve the soluweb (see *Materials* for method).

Leaf C (work one)

1   Trace the pattern onto Vilene.

2   Cut a length of wire to fit around the leaf. Using two strands of **ASC 275** and stab stitch,

couch the wire in place around the edge of the leaf.

3   Cut three pieces of wire double the length of the central vein plus stalk extension and two branches, as shown in the diagram, and fold each piece in half. Starting at **X** and using **FW 2400**, couch part of the longest folded wire in place along the centre vein, working extra stitches at the top of the loop and leaving the remainder to form the stalk extension. Bend the other two folded pieces of wire to fit the vein branches and couch in place.

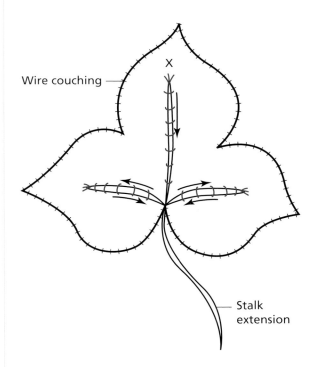

Wire couching

X

Stalk extension

4   Turn the work over. Using **FW 2400**, work a row of close long and short buttonhole stitch over the wire (leaf edge and veins), angling the stitches as shown in the diagram. Fill in the rest of the leaf shape with **FW 2400** in long and short satin stitch.

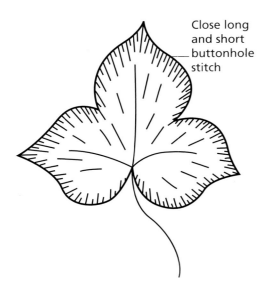

Close long
and short
buttonhole
stitch

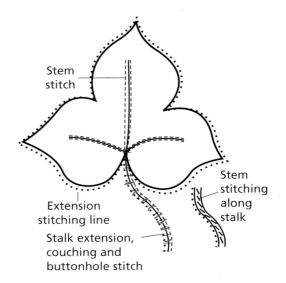

Stem
stitch

Stem
stitching
along
stalk

Extension
stitching line

Stalk extension,
couching and
buttonhole stitch

5 Using **ASC 926**, work three rows of stem stitch along the centre vein and each branch. Carefully cut out the leaf, but do not cut off the wire extension.

6 Place leaf with right side up on a piece of soluweb and pin in place. Using **RAS ecru**, work an extension row of close long and short buttonhole stitch around the leaf as shown in the diagram (above right).

7 Lay the wire extension along the soluweb to form the stalk and couch with two strands of **ASC 926**. Work two rows of close short buttonhole stitch over each wire using two strands of **ASC 926**, so that the rows touch in the centre. With the same thread, work rows of stem stitch on top of the buttonhole stitch up to the edges of the stalk.

8 Cut away the excess soluweb and dissolve the remainder.

Leaf D (work two)

1 Trace the leaf pattern onto Vilene.

2 Cut a length of wire to fit around the leaf and another piece double the length of the centre vein. For the second leaf cut the central piece long enough to form a stalk extension, as for leaf C. Fold the wire for the central vein (and stalk extension) in half. Using two strands of **ASC 275**, couch the wire in place around the leaf edge and along the centre vein, leaving the wire extension on the second leaf.

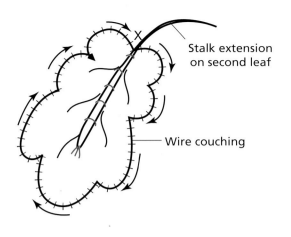

Stalk extension on second leaf

Wire couching

3   Turn the work over. Using **FW 2400**, work close long and short buttonhole stitch over the wire around the edge of the leaf. Fill in the rest of leaf with long and short satin stitch in **FW 2400**. Carefully cut the leaf out and trim excess wire.

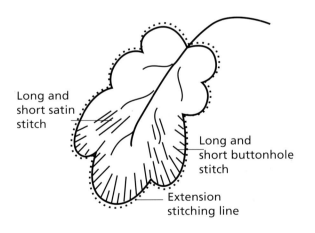

Long and short satin stitch

Long and short buttonhole stitch

Extension stitching line

4   Place the leaf with right side up on a piece of soluweb and pin to hold in place. Using **FS 45**, work an extension row around the leaf edge with close long and short buttonhole stitch, then embroider the centre vein and vein branches in stem stitch on top of the buttonhole stitch. Highlight the leaf by embroidering straight stitches in the same thread at random on top of the cream wool.

5   The second leaf is the same except that in step 3 the excess wire is not trimmed and in step 4 one extension row is worked in **FW 2400**, and then another row on top in **AM 1036**, together with the centre vein and highlights. To form the stalk extension at the bottom of this leaf, couch the protruding wire onto soluweb as for leaf C (step 7), but use **AM 1036**.

6   Dissolve the soluweb.

Leaf E

1   Trace the leaf pattern onto Vilene. Using 26-gauge beading wire, cut a piece to fit around the leaf. Using **FW 2400**, couch the wire in place.

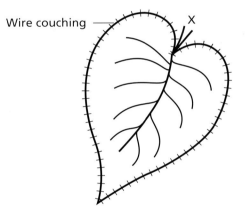

Wire couching

2   Turn the work over and using **FW 2400** embroider close long and short buttonhole stitch over the wire around the edge of the leaf, and then fill in with long and short satin stitch.

3   Carefully cut the leaf out and trim excess wire.

4   Place the leaf right side up on a piece of soluweb and pin to hold in place. Work an extension row around the leaf edge with close long and short buttonhole stitch using **FW 2400**.

5   Using stem stitch, highlight and embroider the centre vein with one strand of **AM 1036**.

6   Dissolve the soluweb.

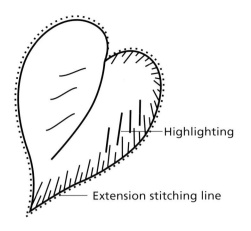

Highlighting

Extension stitching line

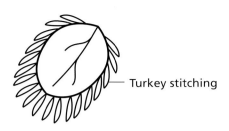

Turkey stitching

Remaining leaves

1   The rest of the leaves are worked in the same way as above, but with varying vein and extension threads. If you prefer more of a beige effect, work more leaves with beige edging.

2   For leaf F, after working the extension row and dissolving the soluweb, work a row of turkey stitches around the edge, using two strands of **FS 45**. Cut the loops and taper them so that they are shorter at the base of the leaf.

3   The following two optional extra leaf patterns can be worked in the same way as the other leaves.

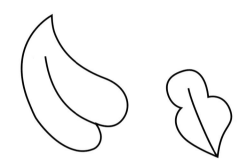

Flowers

There are three flowers, each with five petals. Each petal is worked in the same way, but the colours can be varied according to personal choice. Two flowers are worked in the same colour and the other has additional highlights in one strand of **AM 1036**.

1   Trace the petal pattern five times onto Vilene.

2   Cut 26-gauge wire to fit around the petal shapes, crossing the wire at **X**. Couch the wire around the shapes using two strands of **ASC 275** and stab stitch.

Leaf F

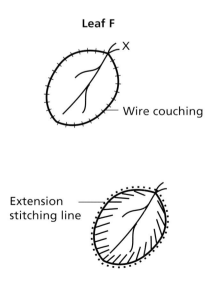

X

Wire couching

Extension stitching line

60

3 Turn the work over. Using one strand of **FW 2400**, work close long and short buttonhole stitch over the wire. Fill in the remainder of the petal with long and short satin stitch in two strands of **FW 2400**.

4 Cut the petal out close to the buttonhole stitching, trimming excess wire. Place right side up on a piece of soluweb and pin to hold in place. Using two strands of **YLI 000**, work an extension row of close long and short buttonhole stitch.

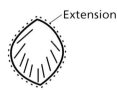

Extension

5 Highlight with straight stitches in **RAS ecru** on top of the wool, fanning out from the bottom of the petal.

Straight stitches fanning out

6 Dissolve the soluweb.

Assembling each flower

1 Place a piece of Vilene in your hoop.

2 Fold three stamens in half, place on the Vilene and secure over the fold with a few stitches in **ASC 275**. Couch a few stitches over the stamens a little further up, leaving about 1 cm (½") loose at the top.

Stamens

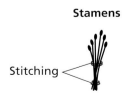

Stitching

3 Using two strands of **FS 45**, work a few turkey stitches around the top of the stamens as shown.

Turkey stitching

4 Attach one strand of **FS 45** at the base of a petal and sew in place close to the turkey stitches. Repeat with the other four petals to form a flower around the turkey stitches. Bend the petals over, cut the loops of the turkey stitches and trim.

5 Trim away the Vilene, leaving a small amount on the back to use for attaching the flowers to the background fabric.

Blossom

1 Trace the blossom pattern below onto Vilene and, using one strand of **ASC 367** and one strand of **ASC 275** together, fill in with turkey stitches. Trim close to the base of the stitching.

2 Sew gathering stitches close to the edge of the Vilene. Pull up to gather and secure the thread on the wrong side of the turkey stitch.

Cut loops

Turkey stitch

Gathering stitch

Berries

There are eight small and three larger berries, all of which are worked in the same way. Cover the small berries with **MH 40123** beads and the larger ones with **MH 00123**.

1   Thread a length of 28-gauge wire through the pebble bead, fold the wire over at the top of the bead, bend back to the bottom of the bead and twist the ends of the wire together, leaving the wire extending below the bead.

2   Now cover the bead with thread. Using two strands of **ASC 275**, take the needle through the bead to the top, leaving a long tail of thread at the bottom. Take the needle back to the bottom of the bead and back up through the centre again. Repeat until the bead is completely covered with thread.

3   Wrap the remaining thread over the wires extending from the bottom of the bead. Fold up a small piece of the wire and twist to secure the thread.

4   Cover the pebble bead with beads, picking up two at a time, and filling in with a single bead if there are any gaps.

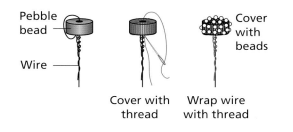

Pebble bead · Wire

Cover with thread · Wrap wire with thread

Cover with beads

Acorns

Work five acorns.

1   Repeat steps 1 to 3 as for the berries, using two strands of **RAS ecru**.

2   Attach a few DBC 22 beads to the centre of the pebble bead and whip stitch one row of **MH 40123** around them.

Small butterfly at top of picture

1   Trace the wing pattern twice onto Vilene. Both wings are worked in the same way.

2   Measure a length of 28-gauge wire to fit around each wing. Couch the wire in place using two strands of **ASC 275**.

3   Turn the work over. Using one strand of **FW 2400**, work close long and short buttonhole stitch over the wire and fill in with long and short satin stitch.

4   Carefully cut the wings out, trimming excess wire.

5   Place the wings right side up on a piece of soluweb and, using **ASC 388**, embroider an extension row of close long and short buttonhole stitch around the edges.

6   Using **AM 1036**, highlight the edges with spaced and varying lengths of buttonhole stitch. Using one strand of **RAS ecru**, highlight the bottom of each wing with straight stitches, fanning out from **X**.

Highlighting

X

7   Dissolve the soluweb.

8   Trace the body of the butterfly onto Vilene. Using two strands of **ASC 380**, fill the shape in with turkey stitches. Cut the loops and trim.

9   Using one strand of **FS 45**, attach the base of one of the wings to the body. Repeat with the second wing, tucking it partially behind the top wing. Cut the butterfly out close to the turkey stitching on the free side of the body, but leaving a small amount on the wing side for attaching to the background fabric.

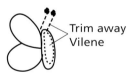

Trim away Vilene

10   To make the first feeler, sew a sequence of beads to the top of the turkey stitching. Secure the thread at the top of the body and pick up three bronze two-cut beads and one size 1.5 cream pearl. Take the needle back down through the bronze beads, leaving the pearl on the end, and secure thread. Repeat for the second feeler.

Butterfly for centre

1   Trace the wings onto a piece of Vilene.

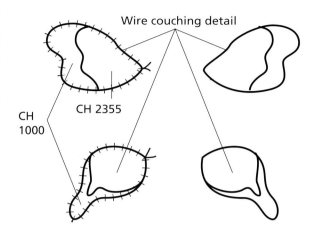

Wire couching detail

CH 2355

CH 1000

2   Cut a length of 28-gauge wire to fit around each wing.

3   Using two strands of **CH 1000** or **CH 2355** (see diagram), couch the wire in place.

4   Turn the work over. Embroider long and short close buttonhole stitch around the wings over the wire and then fill in with long and short satin stitch, using threads as indicated.

5   Using one strand of **AL 303**, highlight the wings with straight stitches on the beige sections.

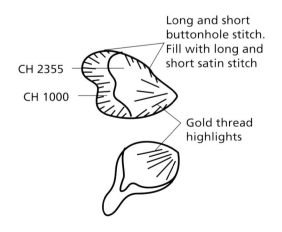

Long and short buttonhole stitch. Fill with long and short satin stitch

CH 2355

CH 1000

Gold thread highlights

6 Cut the wings out close to the buttonholed edge and trim excess wire.

7 Cut a piece of 24-gauge wire the length of the wings, sandwich between each wing and a piece of beige felt, and pin to hold in place.

8 Pick up and sew two or three beads of **DBC 22** through all thicknesses. Trim the felt away.

9 Cut out pieces of felt slightly larger than the wings, pin the embroidered wings and the felt together, and then whip stitch two beads of **DBC 22** around all edges.

10 Trace the body shape onto a piece of beige felt and embroider short close buttonhole stitch around the edge. Using three strands of **ASC 904**, embroider the whole body in turkey stitch. Cut the loops and comb with a small

eyelash brush to fluff up. Cut the felt away close to the buttonholed edge.

Body of butterfly

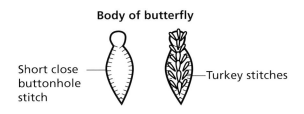

Short close buttonhole stitch — Turkey stitches

11 Attach the wings to another piece of beige felt, leaving a small gap for the body. Stitch the body between the wings.

12 Attach two **MH 00123** beads for the eyes.

13 Trim away the beige felt, leaving a small amount of felt at the back to attach to the centre of your picture.

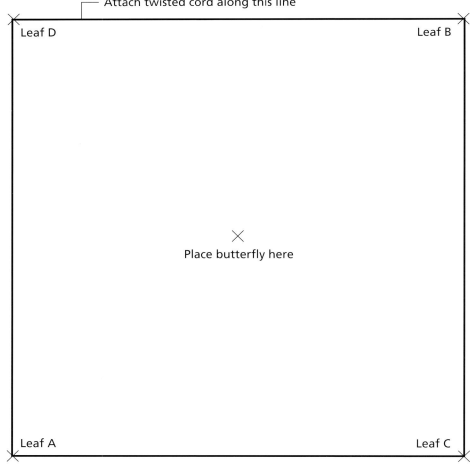

Attach twisted cord along this line

Leaf D
Leaf B

✕
Place butterfly here

Leaf A
Leaf C

To assemble the picture

1   Tack a piece of light-weight Shapewell to the back of the brown silk.

2   Draw the square pattern outline on the silk.

3   Using a combination of six different threads in 3 m lengths, make a thick twisted cord. Sew the twisted cord along the square pattern outline using one strand of any thread. It doesn't matter if the cord doesn't cover the pattern line: any part of the line left uncovered will look like a branch. Use up all the cord by doubling it in places.

4   Neaten and sew the ends of the cord to the background fabric. (The ends can be covered with leaves.)

5   Using one strand of **ASC 275** and a few straight stitches, attach the leaves to the cord, using the photograph as a guide and starting with the corner leaves (A, B, C and D). The leaves with stalk extensions are attached so that the stalk looks as though it is an extension of the cord. Add the flowers and the rest of the leaves.

6   Bend the leaves over to shape them, sewing a slip stitch underneath if needed to hold them in shape. Take the needle through to the back of the background fabric and secure the thread.

7   Sew on the berries, acorns, blossom and the small butterfly.

8 · Sew the large butterfly in the centre or attach with a small piece of double-sided adhesive tape.

Trumpet flower

A dazzling combination of beads and rich colours are worked to create this stunning flower.

WHAT YOU NEED

Thick Vilene, 20 cm × 90 cm (8" × 36")
Soluweb, 20 cm × 90 cm (8" × 36")
26-gauge, 28-gauge and 30-gauge beading
  wire

Finished size 11 cm high × 9 cm wide
  (4½" × 3½")

Threads

Kaalund Yarns Mulberry Silk	Symbol
1 skein S 120 (variegated lavender)	**1**
1 skein S 148 (dark purple and yellow)	**2**
1 skein S 107 (green)	

Kaalund Yarns Fine Wool	
4 skeins 2472 (green)	**3**
1 skein 2470 (variegated lavender)	**4**
1 skein 2442 (dark purple)	**6**
1 skein 2404 (yellow)	**7**

Kaalund Yarns 2-ply Wool	
1 skein 6473 (dark mulberry)	**5**

Anchor Lamé	
1 skein 303 (gold)	**AL 303**

Beads

	Symbol
30 cream pearls, 3 mm	**1**
Delica, size 11	
3 g DBR 34 (gold)	**2**
6g DBC 29 (purple and gold)	**3**
3 g DBC 24 (green)	**4**
3 g gold bugle beads, size 1	**5**

STITCH SYMBOLS

AA	whipped stem stitch
B	feather stitch
C	close short buttonhole stitch
D	close long and short buttonhole stitch
E	long and short satin stitch
F	herringbone stitch
G	detached buttonhole stitch
H	cast-on stitch (15 stitches)
I	French knot

METHOD

The three outer sections of the trumpet flower are embroidered and beaded. Its three lining sections are embroidered in green. At the top of the flower there are three beaded leaves and a twisted cord to hang it up. One strand of thread is used for all embroidery unless otherwise indicated.

Embroidering the outer sections

1   Trace the pattern for the trumpet flower onto three separate pieces of Vilene.

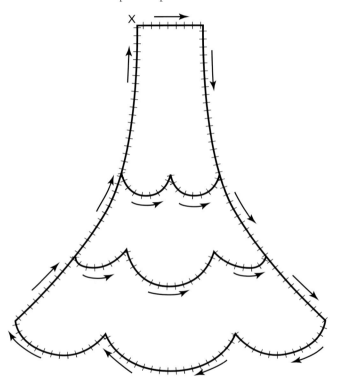

2   For each of the three pattern pieces, cut one length of 26-gauge wire to fit around the outside of the shape starting at **X**, leaving a little extra wire at the top. Cut two lengths of 26-gauge wire to match the internal scalloped lines.

3   Place one pattern piece in a hoop. Using one strand of thread to match each section (see base stitching diagram), couch the wire along the marked lines. Work extra stitches at each sharp bend or point, and then bend the wire

carefully to continue. Repeat with the other two pattern pieces.

4   Turn the work over in the hoop so that the wire is underneath.

5   Using the threads indicated in the diagram, work close short buttonhole stitch over the wire along the sides and top of all three pieces.

6   Starting in the centre at the bottom of the shape and using thread **6**, work long and short close buttonhole stitch over the wire to the left outside edge, making sure the stitch direction is consistent with the shape (as shown in the diagram). Repeat from the centre to the right edge.

7   Using thread **6**, fill in the rest of the bottom section in long and short satin stitch, taking the stitching right up to the edges over the short buttonhole stitch. (This applies to all the embroidery on the flower sections.)

8   Using thread **4**, fill in the middle section with long and short satin stitch.

9   Using long and short satin stitch, fill in the left side of the top section with thread **5** and the right side with thread **7**.

Base stitching

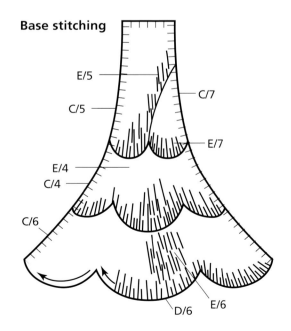

10 Using thread **1**, work a row of double-wrap French knots along the scalloped line between the bottom dark mulberry section and the middle yellow section.

11 Using thread **2**, work herringbone stitch all over the top right (yellow) section. Using thread **1**, work a line of feather stitch down the centre of the top left (dark mulberry) section.

12 On the middle section of the flower, secure six pearls to mark the centres of the flowers. Using thread **1**, work 15 cast-on stitches four times around each pearl to form the four petals.

Top embroidery

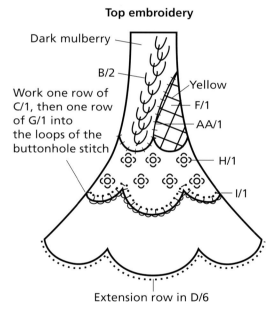

Dark mulberry

B/2

Work one row of C/1, then one row of G/1 into the loops of the buttonhole stitch

Yellow

F/1

AA/1

H/1

I/1

Extension row in D/6

13 Carefully cut out the three shapes close to the buttonholed edge and trim excess wire.

14 Place one of the shapes, right side up, on top of a piece of soluweb, pin and place in an embroidery hoop. Using thread **6**, work an extension row of long and short buttonhole stitch from the embroidered piece onto the soluweb. Repeat for the other two shapes.

15 Cut away as much of the soluweb as possible and dissolve the remainder (see *Materials* for method).

Embroidering the lining sections

1 Trace around the pattern piece onto Vilene.

2 For the lining sections, only the outside of each shape is wired. Cut a length of 28-gauge wire to fit around the shape, starting at **X**, and couch with stab stitches using thread **3**.

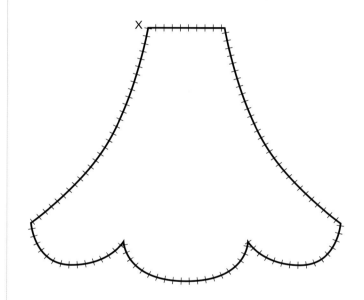

X

3 Using thread **3**, work short close buttonhole stitch along the sides and top of the shape. With the same thread, work long and short buttonhole stitch along the bottom edge and then fill the entire shape in with long and short satin stitch, embroidering right up to the edge of the wire.(See stitching diagram.)

Stitching for lining

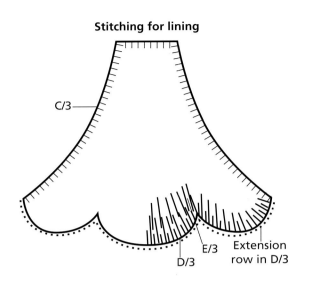

Beading

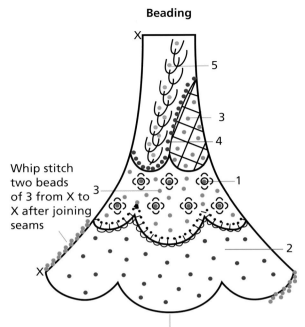

Whip stitch two beads of 3 from X to X after joining seams

Whip stitch three beads of 3 around bottom edge

4 Using one strand of **AL 303**, highlight with random straight stitches on top of the wool.

5 Carefully cut out close to the buttonholed edges.

6 Using thread **3**, work an extension row as for the outer sections of the flower (steps 14 and 15).

7 Repeat steps 1–6 for the other two lining sections.

Beading

Work beading as shown in the diagram.

Assembling the flower

1 Place wrong sides of one top section and one lining section together, matching the patterns at the sides. Using thread **6**, whip stitch together carefully along the bottom edges, and then along the side edges. Leave the top open. If the lining is slightly smaller than the outer sections at the sides, bend the outer shapes to match the lining. Repeat with the other two sections of the flower.

2 For each of the three sections, cut three pieces of wire double the length of the flower, as shown in the diagram. Fold each piece in half and slide between the lining and the outer layer. Trim excess wire.

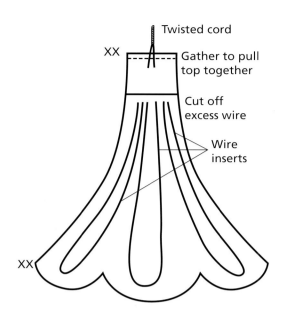

Twisted cord

XX

Gather to pull top together

Cut off excess wire

Wire inserts

XX

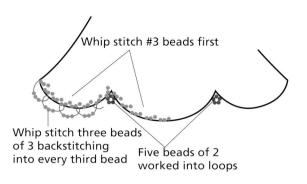

Whip stitch #3 beads first

Whip stitch three beads of 3 backstitching into every third bead

Five beads of 2 worked into loops

3   Cut 2 m (2 yd) of **S 107**, fold in half and make a twisted cord.

4   Using thread **6**, place two of the joined flower sections green sides together. Starting at XX, whip stitch two sections together along the side, using grey beading thread. Join the third section in the same way to form the trumpet flower.

5   Insert the cord in the opening at the top of the flower, secure with running stitch around the top, and then pull up to draw the top together.

Beading the bottom edge

1   Pick up three beads of **3** and whip stitch groups of this combination all the way round the bottom edge. Bead another row by picking up three beads of **3** and, missing two beads from the previous row, taking the needle through the next bead as if working a backstitch. Repeat this until you reach one of the inner points of the scalloped edge, then pick up five beads of **2** and take your needle back into the same spot so that the beads form a loop.

2   Working along the side seams on the outside of the flower, pick up two beads of **3** and whip stitch groups of this combination over the seams. Repeat for the lining seams with two beads of **2**, pulling the green edges as close together as possible.

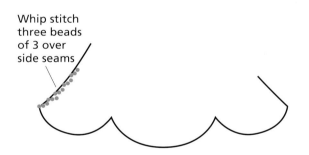

Whip stitch three beads of 3 over side seams

Leaves

1   Trace the leaf pattern onto Vilene. Cut a piece of 30-gauge beading wire to fit around the leaf shape and couch in place. Cut another piece of 30-gauge wire double the length of the centre vein plus a small tail, and fold in half. Using thread 3, couch the wire onto Vilene, working extra stitches at the top of the loop.

2   Turn the work over. Starting at the top of the leaf with thread **3**, work long and short buttonhole stitch along one side and then repeat along the other side. Fill the leaf in with long and short satin stitch in the same thread.

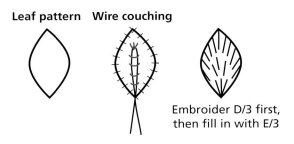

Leaf pattern **Wire couching**

Embroider D/3 first,
then fill in with E/3

Leaf beading

3 Carefully cut the leaf out close to the buttonholed edge and trim excess wire. Pick up and sew groups of three beads of **4** to form veins, then whip stitch one bead of **4** all around the leaf shape.

4 Using thread **3**, attach the leaves to the top of the flower with straight stitches.

Summer berries

This elaborate design brings together luscious berries, dainty flowers, leaves and delicately embroidered insects in a colourful hanging ornament that recalls the warm days of summer.

WHAT YOU NEED

Gold dupion silk, 20 cm × 115/90 cm (8" × 45/36")

Green lawn, 10 cm × 115/90 cm (4" × 45/36")

Vilene, 20 cm × 115 cm (8" × 45")

Light-weight Shapewell (Permashape), 20 cm × 115 cm (8" × 45")

Thin Pellon, 20 cm × 90 cm (8" × 36")

Soluweb, 20 cm × 90 cm (8" × 36")

1 bunch stamens

28-gauge beading wire

30-gauge green covered wire

8 amp electrical fuse wire

Copic markers: lipstick red (R29S), Spanish olive (YG97S), verdigris (G85S)

Cottonwool balls

1 plastic plumbing cap, 6 cm diameter × 2.5 cm deep (2 ⅜" diameter × 1" deep)

Size approximately 13 cm wide × 21 cm long (5" × 8¼")

Threads

Kaalund Fine Wool (FW)
1 skein 2476 (rust and green tones)
1 skein 2415 (green)
1 skein 2451 (green)
1 skein 2422 (dark purple)
1 skein 2428 (purple tones)
1 skein 2426 (rich red)

Kaalund Yarns Fine Mulberry Silk (FS)
1 skein FS 138 (multicoloured)
1 skein FS 102 (green)
1 skein FS 111 (green)
1 skein FS 140 (red)
1 skein FS 36 (gold)
1 skein FS 138 (green)

Kaalund Yarns Indulgence
1 skein tropical berries

Kaalund Yarns Silk Twists — Fine
1 hank tropical berries

Colour Streams Silken Strands (SS)
1 skein 26 (Tuscan olive)
1 skein 21 (purple genie)
1 skein 10 (Venetian sunset)

Colour Streams Exotic Lights (EL)
1 skein 29 (russet)

The Thread Gatherer Silk 'n Colors (SNC)
1 skein 58 (strawflower)
1 skein 18 (terra cotta)

Cascade House Australia (CSS)
1 card Stranded Silk 3995 (fuschia and
   purple tones)

Anchor Stranded Cotton (ASC)
1 skein 47 (red)
1 skein 297 (yellow)

Anchor Lamé (AL)
1 skein 303 (gold)

YLI Silk Floss (YLI)
1 skein 818 (dark purple)
1 skein 00 (natural white)

Beads
Mill Hill (MH)
1 pkt 00367 (black)
1 pkt 02104 (deep red)
1 pkt 00374 (rainbow)

Other beads
3 g Delica DBR 31 (gold), size 11
Red or black glass pebble beads, 5.5 mm
Red or black pony beads, 9 mm
Blue-black or blue-purple seed beads

METHOD

The ornament consists of strawberries, flowers, blackberries, buds and leaves all arranged on top of a tassel with five embroidered insect tabs (dragonfly, ladybird, bee, butterfly and beetle), and is suspended by a twisted cord. Make as many of the fruits, flowers, berries and leaves as you like in a variety of sizes. One strand is used throughout for embroidery unless otherwise indicated.

Strawberries

1   Using the lipstick red Copic marker, trace around the large or small strawberry pattern onto Vilene and colour it in. When dry, place in an embroidery hoop.

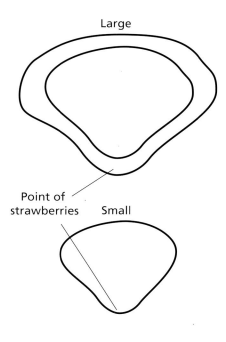

Large

Point of
strawberries   Small

2   Using one strand of **FW 2426**, work close long and short buttonhole stitch around the top and side edges of the shape, and close short buttonhole stitch around the point of the strawberry from a to b. Fill the shape in with long and short satin stitch in the same thread.

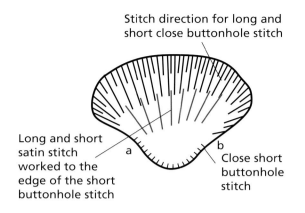

Stitch direction for long and short close buttonhole stitch

Long and short satin stitch worked to the edge of the short buttonhole stitch

a   b

Close short buttonhole stitch

3   Using **FS 140**, work rows of detached chain stitch over the entire shape, placing the anchoring stitches towards the point of the strawberry.

Detached chain stitches

4   Using **FS 36** work a small straight stitch at the base of a few of the detached chain stitches to represent the strawberry seeds.

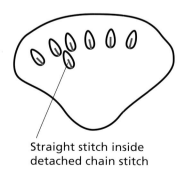

Straight stitch inside detached chain stitch

5   Carefully cut out the strawberry shape as close as possible to the buttonholed edge.

Note. You can vary the strawberries in colour by starting with **FW 2476** at the top then changing to **FW 2426**. Highlight these colours with straight stitches in matching silk thread.

6   Cut a 10 cm (4") length of green covered wire. Fold over one end of the wire approximately 7 mm (¼") and pinch the wire together tightly, leaving a small loop at the top. On the wrong side of the strawberry shape, place the wire loop approximately half-way down in the centre and secure with a few anchoring stitches.

7   Fold the strawberry shape in half over the wire, so that the long edges meet. Using **FW 2426**, slip stitch along this edge and then work a few detached chain stitches in **FS 140** so that the stitches blend.

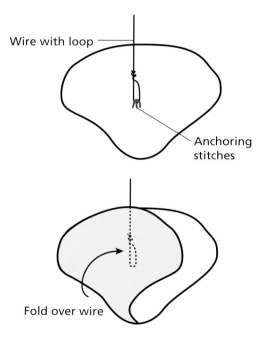

Wire with loop

Anchoring stitches

Fold over wire

8   Fill the embroidered strawberry with cotton-wool around the wire until firm.

9   Using two strands of **FS 140**, work small running stitches around the top of the strawberry. Pull the stitches up and secure the thread.

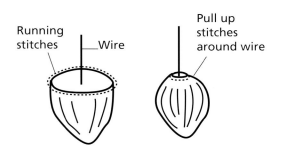

Running stitches | Wire | Pull up stitches around wire

10 Using two strands of **FW 2415**, secure the thread to the top of the strawberry and wrap the thread around the wire tightly for about 7 cm (3"), turning over the end of the wire and twisting to hold the thread firmly.

Strawberry calyx

1 Trace the pattern onto Vilene using the Copic Spanish olive marker and colour the shape in.

2 Using **SS 26**, work close long and short buttonhole stitch around the edges of the shape. Using the same thread, fill the shape in with long and short satin stitch.

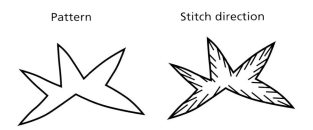

Pattern | Stitch direction

3 Carefully cut the shape out close to the buttonholed edge. If any of the white Vilene is left showing, touch up with the Spanish olive marker.

4 Wrap the calyx around the top of the strawberry and its stem, and sew to the top of the strawberry with **SS 26**.

Strawberry leaves

1 Trace the small or large leaf pattern onto the Vilene with the Spanish olive marker.

2 Cut a length of 8 amp fuse wire to fit the line marked on the pattern, leaving a wire extension for the stem of approximately 3 cm (1¼"). Couch the wire in place using **FW 2415**.

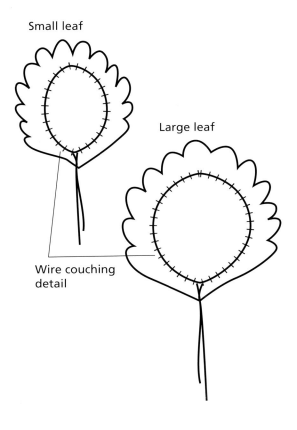

Small leaf

Large leaf

Wire couching detail

3 Turn the work over. Using **FW 2415**, work close long and short buttonhole stitch around the edge of the shape, and then fill in with long and short satin stitch in the same thread.

4 Using **FS 138**, highlight the entire leaf shape with straight stitches worked at random on top of the wool.

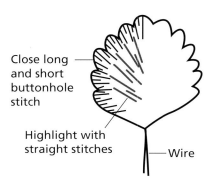

Close long and short buttonhole stitch

Highlight with straight stitches — Wire

5 To add interest, vary the leaves by highlighting some on one side or on a point with **FS 138**.

6 Carefully cut out the shape close to the buttonholed edge. Touch up any white areas still showing around the leaf with the Spanish olive marker.

7 Secure two strands of **FW 2415** to the bottom of the leaf and wrap the wire stem as for the strawberry stems.

Assembling the strawberries

1 To form a bunch of strawberries, hold a few together and wrap one of the wire stems around the other stems to form a single stem.

Wrap one of the wire stems around the others

2 Repeat step 1 to group the leaves together.

3 Add the leaves to the strawberries to form a larger bunch and, using **FW 2415**, secure all the stems together and wrap them with the wool to cover all the wire.

White strawberry flowers

Work five petals for each flower.

1 Trace the petal pattern onto Vilene.

2 Cut a length of 8 amp fuse wire to fit around the edge of the petal. Using two strands of **YLI 00**, couch the wire in place, overlapping it slightly at **X**.

X

3 Turn the work over. Using two strands of **YLI 00**, work close long and short buttonhole stitch over the wire around the edge of the petal. Fill in the rest of the petal with long and short satin stitch using the same thread.

4 Using **ASC 297**, highlight the petal with a few straight stitches fanning out from the base of the petal.

5 Carefully cut out close to the buttonholed edge.

6 Place each petal with right side up on a piece of soluweb and pin to hold. Work an extension row of long and short buttonhole stitch around the petal shape.

7 Dissolve the soluweb (see *Materials*).

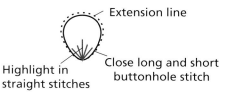

Extension line

Highlight in straight stitches

Close long and short buttonhole stitch

Assembling the strawberry flower

Follow the directions for the flowers in *Cream delight* but use one strand of **ASC 297** and two strands of **YLI 00** together for the turkey stitches.

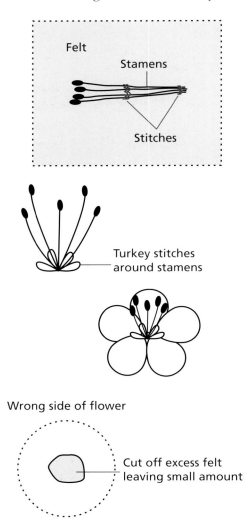

Turkey stitches around stamens

Wrong side of flower

Cut off excess felt leaving small amount

Blackberries

Vary the colour of the blackberries by using more green than purple in some places. Also embroider a couple of berries with two strands of **FW 2476**.

1   Trace the pattern onto Vilene.

2   Work close short buttonhole stitch all the way around the edge of the pattern.
Using one strand of **FW 2428** and one strand of **FW 2442** together, work 8 to 10 granitos stitches over the entire blackberry shape.

Blackberry pattern

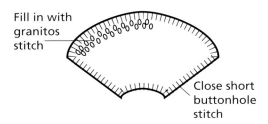

Fill in with granitos stitch

Close short buttonhole stitch

3   Carefully cut the shape out close to the buttonholed edge.

4   Cut and attach a length of wire on the wrong side as for the strawberries.

Attach wire

Wrong side

5   With wrong sides together, fold over and slip stitch together using **FW 138**, pulling in the bottom of the blackberry as you sew.

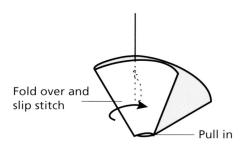

Fold over and slip stitch

Pull in

6   Fill the blackberries with a small amount of cottonwool (they do not need as much as the strawberries, as they are quite thick).

7   Sew a running stitch around the top of the blackberry and pull up tightly. Secure, leaving the excess wire protruding from the centre.

Gathering stitches

8 Secure two strands of **FW 2451** to the top of the blackberry and wrap the wire as for the strawberry.

Blackberry calyx

Make three sepals to form the calyx for each blackberry.

1 Trace sepal pattern onto a piece of green lawn.

2 Using one strand of **FS 111**, work close long and short buttonhole stitch around the shape. Fill in the rest of the shape with long and short satin stitch in the same thread.

Blackberry calyx pattern

Stitch direction

3 Carefully cut out the shape close to the buttonholed edge. Attach the sepals around the wire on the top of the blackberry, with the points facing away from the blackberry.

Placement for calyx

Turkey stitches

4 Using one strand of **SNC 58** and one strand of **SS 26** together, work a few turkey stitches on the top between the calyx and the blackberry, and cut the loops.

Beaded blackberries

Using the 9 mm pony beads and one strand of **FW 2422**, work three or four beaded blackberries following the method for the berries in *Cream delight*. Cover the pony beads with a selection of beads. Wrap the stem of the wire with **FW 2451** and finish off the stem as for the strawberries.

Blackberry leaves

Using **FW 2451** and the verdigris marker, work the blackberry leaves following the directions for the strawberry leaves, and highlight with **FS 102**. The wire is couched down the centre vein only, on the wrong side.

Blackberry leaf pattern

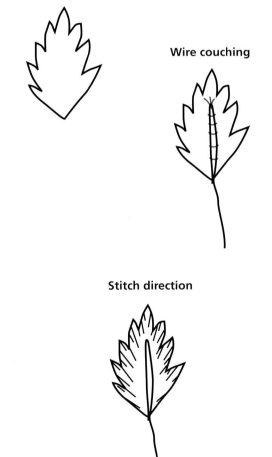

Wire couching

Stitch direction

Blackberry buds

1   Thread a length of 8 amp fuse wire through the pony bead, fold the wire over at the top of the bead, bend back to the bottom of the bead and twist the ends of the wire together, leaving the wire extending below the bead.

2   Cover the entire bead with **FS 138** or **FW 2428**. Secure two strands of **FW 2451** at the base of the bud and wrap wire stem with wool to cover.

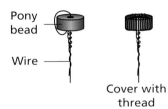

Pony bead
Wire
Cover with thread

Assembling the blackberries and buds

Follow the directions for the strawberries to assemble the blackberries and buds.

Dragonfly tab

1   Trace the design onto the right side of the silk fabric. Tack a piece of light-weight Shapewell to the wrong side.

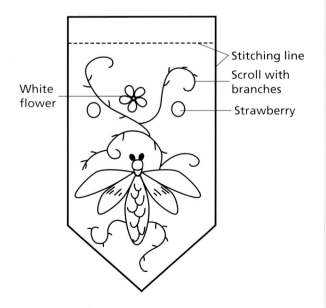

Stitching line
Scroll with branches
Strawberry
White flower

2   Embroider the dragonfly's body with one strand of **FW 2442** in satin stitch.

3   Work the wings in satin stitch with two strands of **SS 21**.

4   Using one strand of **SS 10**, highlight the upper wings on top of the wool with straight stitches fanning out from the body. Highlight the lower wings similarly, using one strand of **SS 26**.

5   Using one strand of **AL 303** and straight stitches, highlight the top and bottom wings again, fanning out from the body on top of the previous embroidery.

6   On the body, work feather stitch on top of the wool using one strand of **AL 303**. Work two straight stitches over the wool near the neck.

7   Using one strand of **FW 2442**, fill in the head with approximately five straight stitches. Attach two small black seed beeds for the eyes.

8   Outline the whole dragonfly with one strand of **AL 303** in stem stitch.

9   For the strawberries, see separate instructions on page 85.

10 The white flowers are worked in the same way for all tabs. Using two strands of **YLI 00**, work 10 granitos stitches to form the petals of the flower. Sew two gold (**DBR 3**) beads to the centre of each flower. Using one strand of **AL 303**, embroider fly stitch around the tips of the petals.

11 The scroll embroidery is worked in the same way for all tabs. Using one strand of **AL 303**, embroider the main scroll lines in whipped stem stitch, and then add small straight stitches branching out from the scroll.

Ladybird tab

1   Trace the design onto the right side of the silk fabric. Tack a piece of light-weight Shapewell to the wrong side.

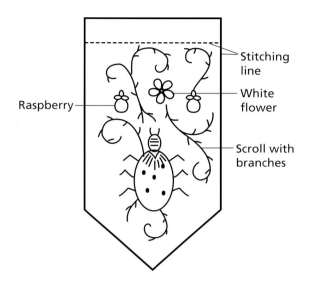

2   Using two strands of **ASC 47**, fill in the body of the ladybird with long and short satin stitch.

3   With small straight stitches in **YLI 818**, work the dots on the ladybird's body.

4   Using two strands of **YLI 818**, fill in the head section with straight stitches and embroider two straight stitches for the feelers .

5   Embroider the legs with straight stitches using two strands of **YLI 818**.

6   Using one strand of **AL 303**, highlight the body with straight stitches on top of the **ASC 47**, fanning out from the back of the neck down onto the body.

7   Outline the whole ladybird in stem stitch with one strand of **AL 303**.

8   To embroider the raspberries, use one strand of **YLI 818** and one strand of **ASC 47** together to fill the raspberry shape with French knots. Using one strand of **SS 26**, embroider straight stitches to form the leaves at the top of the raspberries.

9   For flower and scrolls, see dragonfly tab, steps 10 and 11.

Bee tab

1   Trace the design onto the right side of the silk fabric. Tack a piece of light-weight Shapewell to the wrong side.

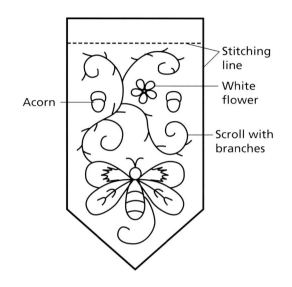

2   Using **EL 29**, fill the body of the bee with straight stitches and the head with French knots.

3   Using one strand of **SNC 58**, fill the four wings with long and short satin stitch. Using one strand of **SNC 18**, highlight the top wings with straight stitches, fanning out from the body.

4   Using one strand of **YLI 818**, embroider a few more straight stitches on the wings close to the head.

5   Using one strand of **SS 26**, embroider feather stitch on the lower wings.

6   Using one strand of **SS 26** and one strand **AL 303** together, embroider straight stitches across the body of the bee as shown.

7   Outline the whole bee in stem stitch with one strand of **AL 303**.

8   To embroider each acorn, work straight stitches in **EL 29**. Using two strands of **SS 26**, embroider French knots at the top of the acorn.

9   For flower and scrolls, see dragonfly tab, steps 10 and 11.

Butterfly tab

1   Trace the design onto the right side of the silk fabric. Tack a piece of light-weight Shapewell to the wrong side.

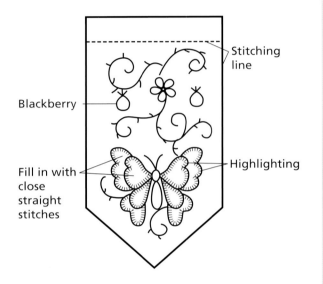

2   Using two strands of **SS 21**, fill the body and head of the butterfly with straight stitches. Embroider a few turkey stitches on top of these stitches in the same thread.

3   Using one strand of **CSS 3995**, embroider close straight stitches on the wing sections closest to the body. Using one strand of **SNC 18**, fill the outer section of the wings to the tips with close straight stitches.

4   Highlight the tips of the wings with straight stitches using one strand of **YLI 818**. Using one strand of **AL 303**, highlight with more straight stitches on top of this embroidery, fanning out from the body.

5   Using **AL 303**, embroider the feelers in straight stitch with a French knot on the end.

6   For the two blackberries, use two strands of **SNC 18** and one strand of **SS 21** together to fill the shape in with French knots. Using one strand of **SS 26**, embroider straight stitches to form the small leaves at the top of the blackberries.

7   For flower and scrolls, see dragonfly tab, steps 10 and 11.

Beetle tab

1   Trace the design onto the right side of the silk fabric. Tack a piece of light-weight Shapewell to the wrong side.

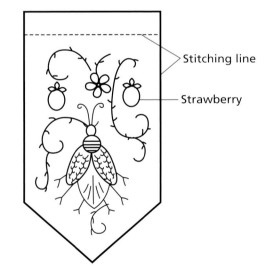

2   Using two strands of **SNC 58**, fill in the bottom part of the beetle's body with close long and short satin stitch.

3   Fill in the wings with two strands of **SS 26** in satin stitch. Using one strand of **AL 303**, work feather stitch on top of the **SS 26**.

4   Using **YLI 818**, embroider the head and feelers in straight stitches with one strand, and the legs in fly stitch with two strands.

5   Using **AL 303**, outline the beetle's body with stem stitch and repeat fly stitches on the legs.

At the bottom of the beetle, work a few straight stitches on top of the **SNC 58**.

6 For flower and scrolls, see dragonfly tab, steps 10 and 11.

7 For strawberries, see below.

Strawberries on the tabs

1 Using two strands of **ASC 47**, fill the strawberry shapes with granitos stitches. Use one strand of **AL 303** to embroider a few straight stitches on the top to represent seeds.

2 Using one strand of **AL 303**, work a few straight stitches on the top of the strawberries to form the leaves.

Assembling the tabs

1 Cut away the Shapewell (but not the silk) to the finished size of the tab. Trim the silk 1 cm (½") larger all round.

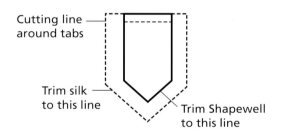

Cutting line around tabs

Trim silk to this line

Trim Shapewell to this line

2 Fold the silk over to the wrong side of the tab and tack in place around the edges.

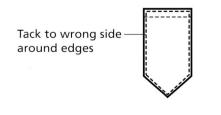

Tack to wrong side around edges

3 Trace the outline of the tab design onto the right side of a plain piece of silk fabric. Tack a piece of light-weight Shapewell to the wrong side. Trim the silk 1 cm (½") larger all round. Repeat step 2.

4 Place the embroidered and plain pieces together with Shapewell sides facing, matching the points, and pin to hold in place.

5 Join together by whip stitching one **MH 00374** bead around the edge, catching both tab pieces and leaving the top open.

6 Repeat steps 1–5 for all tabs.

Making the tassel cover

1 Cut the larger circle of the tassel top pattern from the silk and the smaller circle from the Pellon. Adjust the pattern if the top of the tassel you are making is larger or smaller (make sure you purchase a plastic plumbing cap to match). Tack the silk and Pellon together.

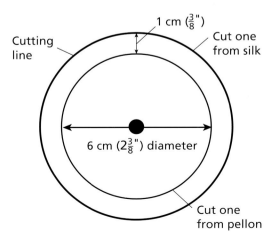

1 cm (⅜")

Cutting line

Cut one from silk

6 cm (2⅜") diameter

Cut one from pellon

2   Using the pattern at the bottom of the page, cut two bands of silk and one of Pellon.

3   Tack the Pellon band and one silk band together.

4   With right sides together, fold the strip in half and sew the side seam.

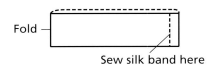

Fold

Sew silk band here

5   With right sides together, pin the strip around the edge of the circle and tack in place. Place the right side of the second silk band to the wrong side of circle, sandwiching the circle between the two silk band pieces, and tack in place. Sew all layers together by hand with small backstitches along the stitching line.

6   Fold the inside of the band out of the way and pin the tabs around the bottom edge of the band. Tack and sew the tabs to the strip by hand with small backstitches along the stitching line.

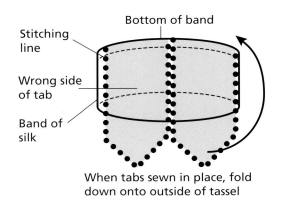

Bottom of band

Stitching line

Wrong side of tab

Band of silk

When tabs sewn in place, fold down onto outside of tassel

7   Fold the inside of the band down, turning under a seam allowance at the bottom, and slip stitch over the raw edges of the front section.

8   Make a hole for the cord in the centre of the circle through the Pellon and the silk.

9   Whip stitch one **MH 00374** bead around the top of the band. Whip stitch two blue-black or blue-purple seed beads along the bottom edge of the band.

Pattern for tassel band

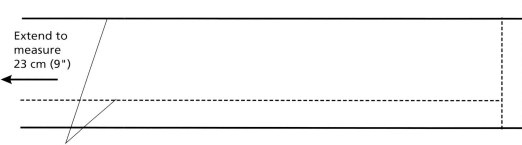

Extend to measure 23 cm (9")

Stitching lines

Assembling the tassel

1   Drill a hole in the centre of the plastic plumbing cap.

2   Make the bottom part of the tassel by cutting the hank of Kaalund Yarns Silk Twists into three pieces, as follows (see diagram). Tie the hank at each end through the loop, then tie the hank in the centre securely. Cut halfway between each of the outer ties and the centre tie (two cuts) to divide the hank into three sections. Tie the three sections together securely to form a tassel. At this stage it will probably be uneven at the bottom, but you can trim this level when the tassel is complete. When trimmed, the finished length of the tassel is approximately 18 cm (7").

3   Make a chunky twisted cord with the full skein of Indulgence and attach the cord to the top of the tassel securely.

4   Place the completed silk cover over the top of the plastic cap, and pull the cord through the plastic and silk cover so that the tassel fits inside.

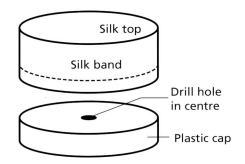

Silk top

Silk band

Drill hole in centre

Plastic cap

5   Sew the cord to the silk cover around the hole.

6   Attach groups of strawberries, blackberries, flowers and leaves to the top of the tassel with a few anchoring stitches over the wire, letting some of the berries hang over the edge.

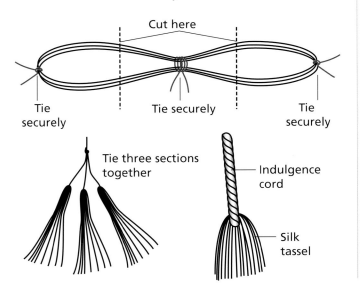

Cut here

Tie securely

Tie securely

Tie securely

Tie three sections together

Indulgence cord

Silk tassel

Cornucopia

A cornucopia is a horn that is filled to overflowing with produce as a symbol of abundance. Here, the design itself is cornucopian, richly embroidered and encrusted with a wonderful variety of multicoloured threads and beads.

WHAT YOU NEED

Coffee-coloured dupion silk (or colour of your choice), 25 cm × 115/90 cm (10" × 45/36")

Thick Vilene, 25 cm × 115 cm (10" × 45")

Medium-weight Shapewell (Permashape), 25 cm × 115 cm (10" × 45")

Thin Pellon, 25 cm × 90 cm (10" × 36")

24-gauge and 28-gauge beading wire

Finished size 16.5 cm × 8 cm (6½" × 3¼")

Threads

Kaalund Yarns Fine Wool	Symbol
1 skein 2442 (purple)	**1**
1 skein 2404 (yellow)	**2**
1 skein 2472 (green)	**3**
1 skein 2487 (multicoloured)	**4**

Kaalund Yarns Mulberry Silk	
1 skein S 148 (multicoloured)	**5**
1 skein S 11 (mulberry)	**6**
1 skein S 08 (yellow)	**7**
1 skein S 120 (multicoloured lavender)	**8**
1 skein S 142 (soft multicoloured)	**9**
1 skein S 133 (green)	**10**

Kaalund Yarns 2-ply Wool	
1 skein 6473 (mulberry)	

Anchor Lamé (AL)	
1 skein 303 (gold)	

Beads

Delica, size 11	Symbol
8 g DBC 29 (multicoloured purple)	**1**
4 g DBC 27 (green)	**2**
4 g DBR 902 (pink)	**3**
4 g DBR 610 (purple)	**4**
4 g DBR 34 (gold)	**5**
4 g DBR 629 (pale mauve)	**8**

Other beads	
6 g gold bugle beads, size 1 (2 mm)	**6**
3 fuchsia bicones, 4 mm	**7**
1 faceted round dark turquoise (AB) crystal, 4 mm	**9**
4 crystal drops, 6 mm	**10**
3 light amethyst bicones, 5 mm	**11**
1 amethyst crystal drop, 6 mm	

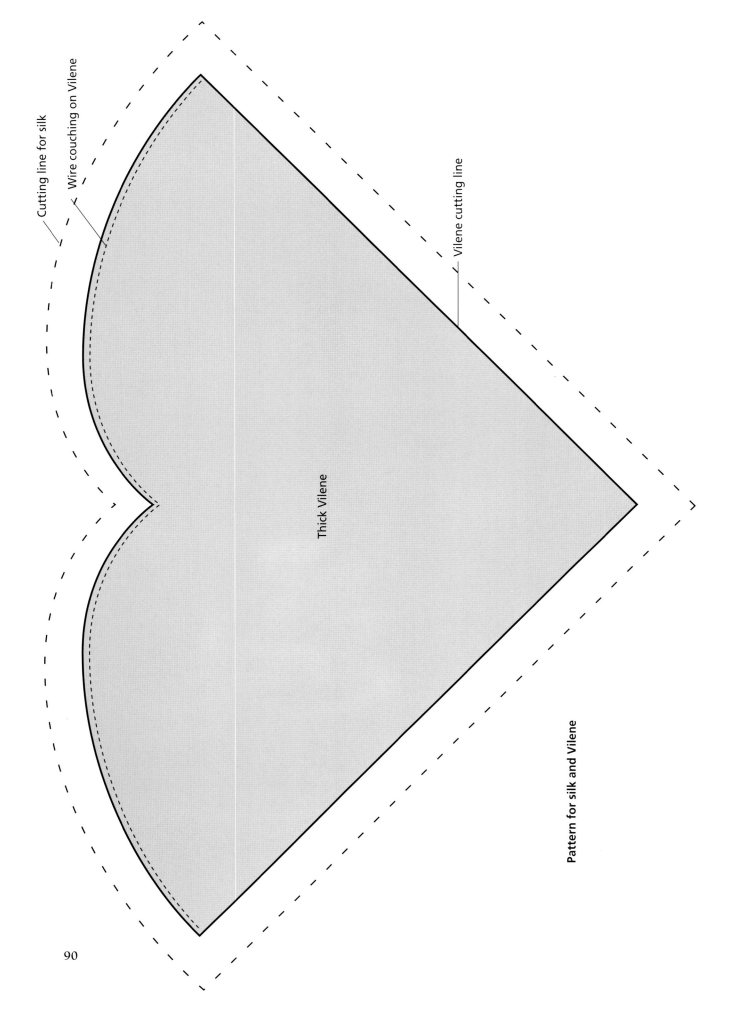

Cutting line for silk

Wire couching on Vilene

Vilene cutting line

Thick Vilene

Pattern for silk and Vilene

90

Embroidery diagram

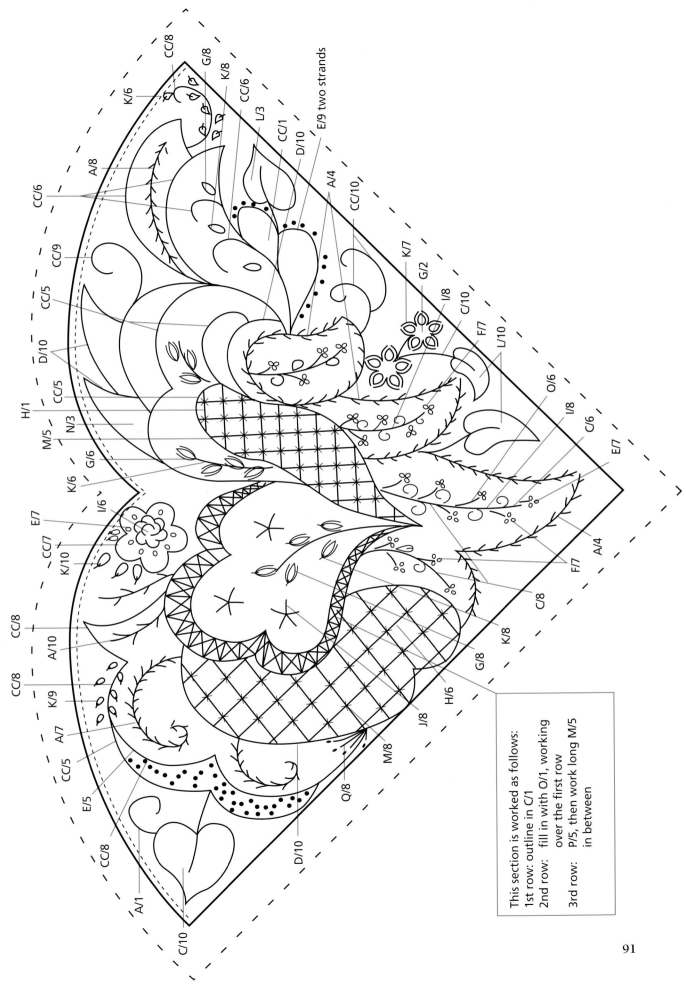

This section is worked as follows:
1st row: outline in C/1
2nd row: fill in with O/1, working over the first row
3rd row: P/5, then work long M/5 in between

91

STITCH SYMBOLS

A   feather stitch

B   chain stitch

BB   whipped chain stitch

C   stem stitch

D   double knot stitch

E   French knot

F   colonial knot

G   granitos stitch (10 stitches)

H   laid stitches

I   cast-on stitch (15 stitches)

J   spider stitch

K   detached chain stitch

L   close fly stitch

M   cross stitch

N   long and short satin stitch

O   straight stitches

Q   pistil stitch

METHOD

The cone is worked on the bias of the fabric. If you are embroidering the same design on a bag flap, it can be worked on the straight grain. One strand of thread is used for embroidery unless otherwise indicated.

1   Trace the pattern onto the silk, including the main design lines, dots, flower and leaf positions etc from the embroidery diagram. Leave enough space around the shape on the silk so that you can work in a hoop. Place a piece of Shapewell under the silk and tack in place.

2   Work the embroidery referring to the stitch and thread symbols, and then the beading following the beading symbols (see *What you need*).

3   When the embroidery and beading are complete, place a piece of Pellon behind the shape. Using one strand of **AL 303**, work lots of small straight stitches at random around all the embroidery.

4   Using one strand of **AL 303**, work five straight stitches on top of the previous embroidery, coming out of the centre of the spider stitch.

Assembling

1   Cut the shape out along the silk cutting line. Carefully trim away the Pellon and Shapewell to the exact size of the cone.

2   On the wrong side, fold the raw edges of the silk over onto the Pellon, clipping in the centre shown, and tack in place close to the outside edges.

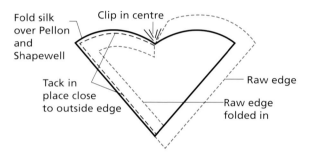

Fold silk over Pellon and Shapewell

Clip in centre

Tack in place close to outside edge

Raw edge

Raw edge folded in

3   Cut out another piece of silk on the bias for the lining.

4   Trace the cornucopia pattern onto a piece of thick Vilene, following the Vilene cutting line. Using beading thread or sewing thread, couch a piece of 24-gauge beading wire around the line marked at the top of the pattern, making sure that the shape matches the embroidered shape. Adjust if necessary before cutting the excess wire off.

5   Cut out the wired shape and place with the wire side up onto the lining silk. Fold the raw edges of the silk over onto the Vilene and tack all round close to the edges.

6   Place the wrong sides of the embroidered and lining pieces together, matching the top edges, and whip stitch the two pieces together along the top.

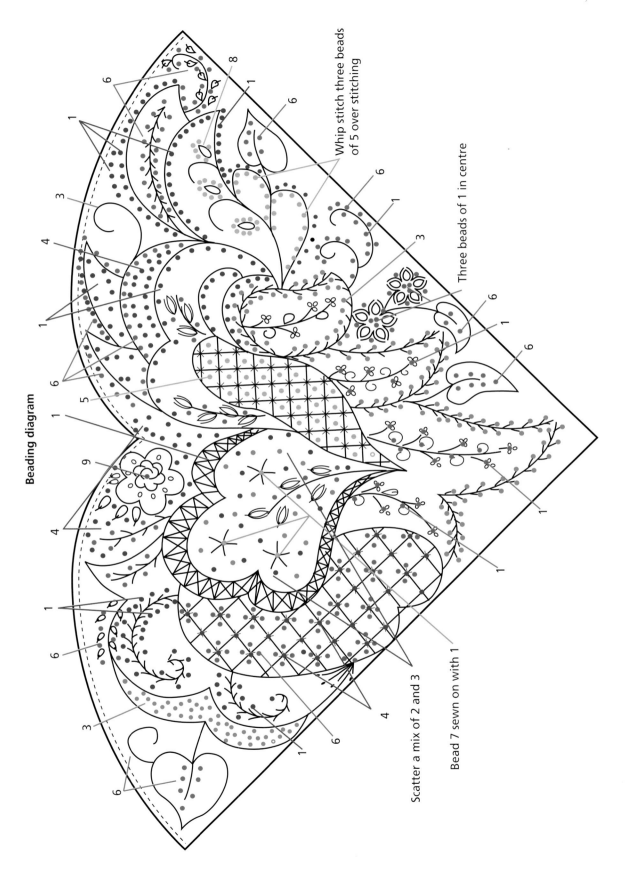

Beading diagram

Whip stitch three beads
of 5 over stitching

Three beads of 1 in centre

Scatter a mix of 2 and 3

Bead 7 sewn on with 1

Cornucopia

93

Silk tab pattern

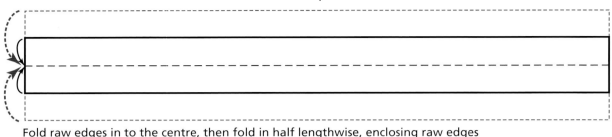

Fold raw edges in to the centre, then fold in half lengthwise, enclosing raw edges

7   Fold the cornucopia with the lining on the inside so that the back edges meet. Whip stitch the back seam of the lining and then the outside back seam, leaving a small opening at the top to insert the tab.

Beaded tab

1   Cut the tab pattern out of the silk. Fold the long raw edges into the centre and then fold in half lengthwise.

2   Down each long edge of the tab, whip stitch two beads of **1**, then one bead of **6**. Whip stitch one bead of **1** lengthwise down the centre of the tab.

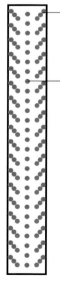

Whipstitch two beads of 1, then one bead of 6

Whipstitch one bead of 1 down centre lengthwise

3   Fold the tab in half to form a loop and insert in the opening left between the lining and outside of the cone at the back. Secure in place with a few stitches and whip stitch the opening closed. Whip stitch a line of gold bugle beads (**6**) down the back seam.

Whip stitch gold bugle beads (6) over the back seam

Dimensional leaves (work three)

1   Trace the leaf pattern onto Vilene.

2   Cut a length of 28-gauge beading wire to fit around the leaf shape, crossing the wire slightly at **X**.

3   Using one strand of thread **3**, couch the wire around the edge of the leaf.

Leaf pattern and couching detail

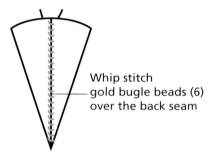

4   Turn the work over and, using the same thread, work close long and short buttonhole around the edge over the wire, then fill in with long and short satin stitch.

**Stitch
direction**

5   Using **AL 303**, highlight with straight stitches on top of the satin stitch.

Highlights

6   Carefully cut the leaf out close to the buttonholed edge and trim excess wire.

7   Whip stitch two beads of **2** around the edge of the leaf. Pick up three of the same beads and sew in place to form each of the veins.

**Beading for veins and
around edge of leaf**

8   Sew the leaves in position at top of the cone.

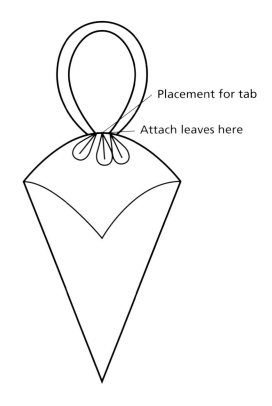

Placement for tab

Attach leaves here

Crystal tassel

Sew crystals to the bottom of the cone in varying lengths. Use a combination of one of **6**, one of **11**, then a crystal drop (**10**), and vary the length by occasionally adding an extra one of **6** at the beginning. Sew a few beads of **1** around the point of the cone.

Splendid slipper

This sumptuous decorative slipper is lavishly embroidered and beaded, and then embellished with flowers, beaded berries and leaves, making it an exquisite gift for a special person.

WHAT YOU NEED

Natural colour wool felt, 25 cm × 25 cm (10" × 10")

Thick Vilene, 25 cm × 90 cm (10" × 36")

Small teddy bear filling pellets, small quantity of cream or white

Cottonwool for filling

5 cm (2") length of 6 mm (⅜") dowel

26-gauge and 28-gauge beading wire

Finished size 18 cm long × 11 cm high (7⅛" × 4⅜")

Threads

Colour Streams	*Symbol*
3 skeins Silken Strands 18 (antique ivory)	**1**
1 skein Exotic Lights 18 (antique ivory)	**2**
1 skein Ophir 18 (antique ivory)	**3**
8 m (8 yd) of 4 mm silk ribbon 18 (antique ivory)	**4**

Cascade House Australia	
2 cards Stranded Silk 1000 (cream)	**5**

Anchor Lamé	
1 skein 303 (gold)	**6**

Beads

Delica, size 11	*Symbol*
6 g DBR 832 (mauve)	**1**
6 g DBR satin mix	**2**
3 g DBR 211 (cream)	**3**

Other beads	
3 g two-cut pale pink (AB), 2 mm	**4**
3 g cream or white sequins, 3 mm	**5**
3 white or cream Mill Hill pebble beads	

Crystals	
4 round faceted AB crystals, 4 mm	**6**
2 crystal flowers, 4 mm	**7**
1 crystal flower, 6 mm	**8**
1 clear heart-shaped crystal	**9**

Pearls	
3 cream pearls, 5 mm	**10**
7 cream pearls, 2.5 mm	**11**

STITCH SYMBOLS

A   stem stitch

AA   whipped stem stitch

B   French knot

C   granitos stitch (8 stitches)

D   laid stitch

E   cross stitch

F   small ribbon stitch

G   feather stitch

H   detached chain stitch

I   close fly stitch

J   straight stitch

K   close short buttonhole stitch

L   pistil stitch

M   herringbone stitch

N   cast-on stitch (8 stitches)

O   long and short satin stitch

METHOD

Stitching and beading diagrams for the slipper are provided in two stages to make them easier to follow, but first trace the whole design from the main pattern. Use two strands of thread unless otherwise indicated.

Embroidery and beading

1. Trace the slipper shape twice onto the right side of the felt.

2. Cut around the outside of shape but leave the top opening of the slipper uncut (see cutting line marked on diagram).

3. Place right sides together and, allowing 3 mm (⅛") seams, join the slipper along the front seam, either by hand with backstitch or by machine.

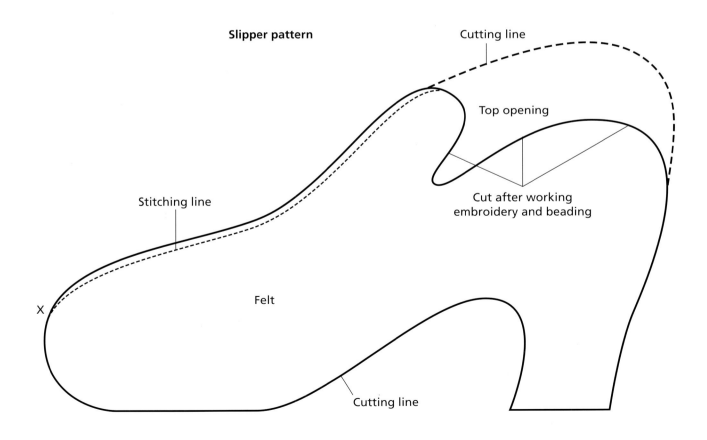

Slipper pattern

Cutting line

Top opening

Cut after working embroidery and beading

Stitching line

X

Felt

Cutting line

Main pattern

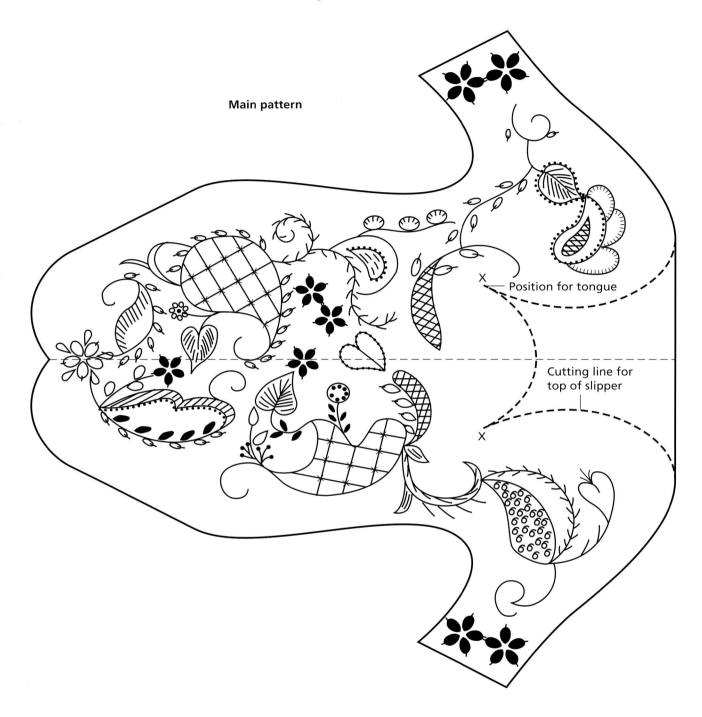

X — Position for tongue

Cutting line for
top of slipper

4 Open the slipper out to the right side and trace the main lines of the embroidery onto the slipper.

5 Work the embroidery and the beading following the stitching and beading diagrams and referring to the symbols (see *What you need* and *Stitch symbols*).

6 Sew small sequins and crystal flowers on the slipper with one bead of **3**.

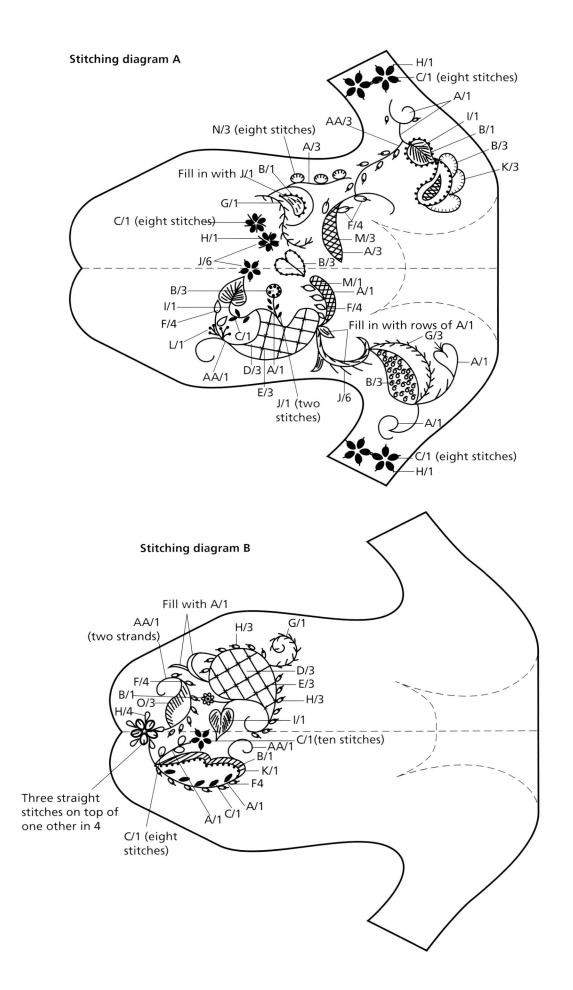

Stitching diagram A

H/1
C/1 (eight stitches)
A/1
N/3 (eight stitches)
AA/3
I/1
B/1
A/3
B/3
B/1
Fill in with J/1
K/3
G/1
C/1 (eight stitches)
H/1
F/4
J/6
M/3
A/3
B/3
B/3
M/1
I/1
A/1
F/4
F/4
Fill in with rows of A/1
L/1
G/3
C/1
A/1
AA/1
B/3
D/3 A/1
E/3
A/1
J/1 (two stitches)
J/6
C/1 (eight stitches)
H/1

Stitching diagram B

Fill with A/1
AA/1 (two strands)
H/3
G/1
F/4
D/3
B/1
E/3
O/3
H/3
H/4
I/1
AA/1
C/1 (ten stitches)
B/1
K/1
F4
Three straight stitches on top of one other in 4
A/1 C/1
A/1
C/1 (eight stitches)

101

Beading diagram A

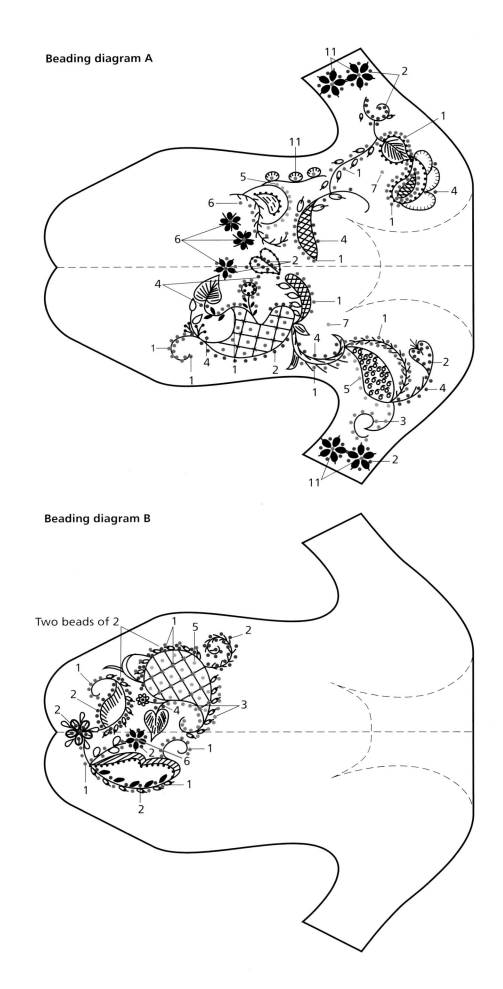

Beading diagram B

Two beads of 2

102

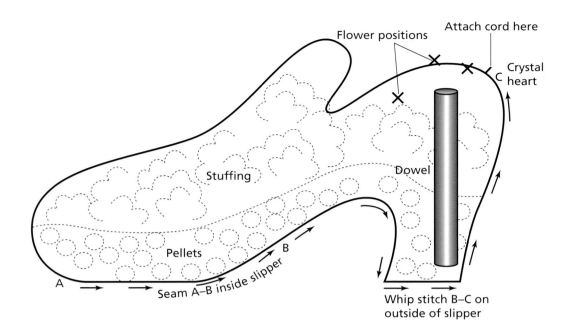

Flower positions · Attach cord here

Crystal heart

C

Dowel

Stuffing

Pellets

B

A

Seam A–B inside slipper

Whip stitch B–C on outside of slipper

Assembling the slipper

1. Remove any trace markings by sponging with cold water.

2. Placing right sides together and, allowing 3 mm (⅛") seams, sew from **A** to **B**.

3. At the toe make a small fold and sew across. Turn to the right side.

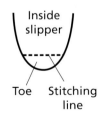

Inside slipper

Toe · Stitching line

4. Cut a piece of felt from the pattern for the tongue of the slipper. Cut out the top opening of the slipper along the cutting line (see main pattern). With wrong sides together and using one strand of **1**, whip stitch these two pieces together around the top, from **X** to **X**.

Slipper tongue pattern

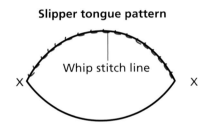

Whip stitch line

X   X

5. Using one strand of **1** and keeping stitches close together, whip stitch the rest of the slipper seam from **B** to **C** (see slipper diagram above).

6. Push the two points at the bottom of the heel to the inside and sew in place with a couple of stitches. This will round the bottom of the heel.

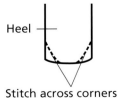

Heel

Stitch across corners

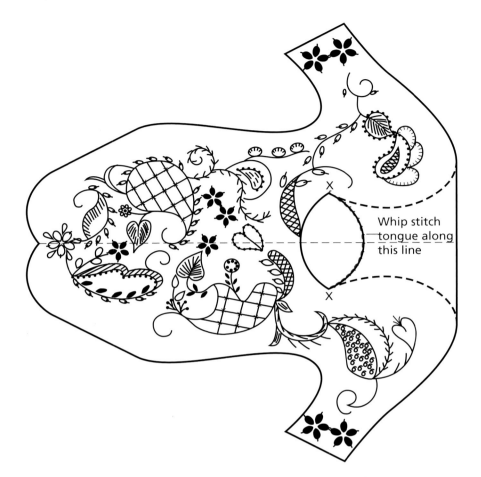

Whip stitch tongue along this line

7   Place pellets in the heel and along the bottom of the shoe. Push the piece of dowel inside the heel (the pellets will keep it straight). Fill the rest of the slipper with cottonwool until firm. Test the slipper to see if it will stand. If it will not, adjust the filling.

8   Cut 2 m (2 yd) lengths of thread **2** and **AL 303**, and make a twisted cord. Sew in place at the back of the slipper with the raw edges inside the slipper.

9   Close the top of the slipper behind the tongue by pulling this section together firmly with whip stitches.

10 Pick up two beads of **1** and whip stitch over the underneath seam, down the back seam of heel, and then around the bottom of the heel.

Ribbon bow

This is made from two half-bow shapes.

1   Trace the half-bow pattern onto Vilene. Cut a length of 26-gauge wire to fit around the shape, from **X** to **X**. Using two strands of **5**, couch wire in place with stab stitches from **X** to **X**.

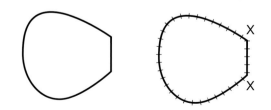

2   Turn the work over. Using three strands of **1**, work close short buttonhole stitch over the wire, leaving a slight gap between the buttonholed edge and the wire.

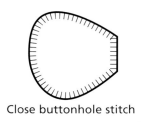

Close buttonhole stitch

3   Using 4 mm ribbon and starting at **a**, embroider long and short satin stitch down one side of the bow, bringing the needle up between the previously worked buttonhole stitch and the wire. Fill the rest of the shape with the ribbon in long and short satin stitch, taking the needle into the ribbon stitches of the first row.

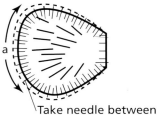

a

Take needle between buttonholed edge and wire

4   Using one strand of **AL 303**, highlight with straight stitches at random, fanning out from the centre of the bow.

5   Repeat steps 1–4 with the other half of the bow.

6   Cut the two half-bow shapes close to the buttonholed edge.

7   Whip stitch two beads of **2** around the half-bow shapes as shown.

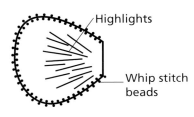

Highlights

Whip stitch beads

8   Place the two half-bow shapes right sides together and sew a few stitches at the centre of the bow to join.

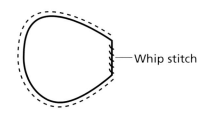

Whip stitch

9   Open the bow out. Secure the 6 mm crystal flower at the centre of the bow. Pick up and sew five beads of **1** in loops around the flower.

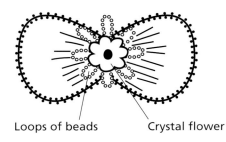

Loops of beads   Crystal flower

10   Attach the bow to the top front of the slipper.

Flowers

There are three flowers, each with four petals, worked in thread and ribbon.

1   Trace the petal pattern onto Vilene

2   Cut lengths of 28-gauge wire to fit around the petal.

3   Using two strands of **5**, couch the wire in place, overlapping slightly at **X**.

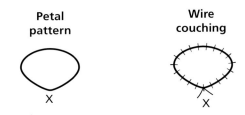

Petal pattern   Wire couching

X   X

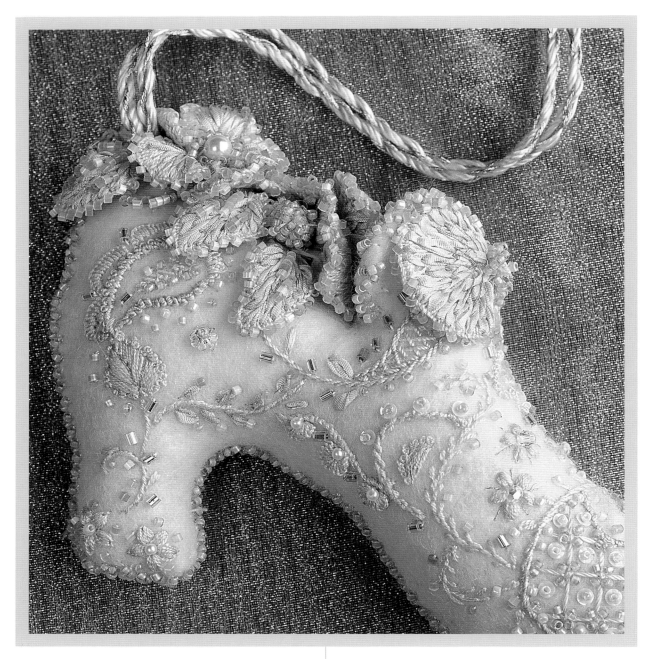

4   Turn the work over. Using two strands of **5**, work long and short buttonhole stitch over the wire around the petal, starting at the centre and working in one direction, and then from the centre in the other direction. Fill the shape in with long and short satin stitch in the same thread.

Long and short
buttonhole stitch

Long and short
satin stitch

5 Using one strand of **1**, highlight the petal by working straight stitches on top of the satin stitch.

6 With 4 mm ribbon, work straight stitches fanning out from the bottom of the petal to approximately three-quarters of the way up the petal.

Ribbon

Highlight with AL 303

7 Repeat steps 1–6 for all petals.

8 Carefully cut the petals out as close as possible to the buttonholed edge.

9 Whip stitch two beads of **2** around the edge of each petal.

10 Place a piece of Vilene in the hoop and, using small straight stitches, sew the flower petals to the Vilene to form a flower, with the petals touching at the centre.

11 Stitch a 5 mm pearl (**10**) in the centre of the flower. Pick up seven beads of **1** and sew four loops around the pearl.

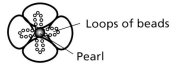

Flower with four petals

Loops of beads

Pearl

12 Cut the flowers out, leaving a small amount of Vilene on the back to attach them to the slipper.

Leaves

There are five leaves.

1 Trace around the leaf pattern onto Vilene.

2 Cut a length of 28-gauge wire to fit around the leaf shape, overlapping the wires slightly at **X**.

3 Using two strands of **5**, couch the wire onto the Vilene.

4 Turn the work over. Using two strands of **1** and one strand of **5** in the same needle, work close short buttonhole stitch over the wire, taking the needle slightly beyond the wire shape. Using 4 mm ribbon (**4**), work long and short satin stitch as for the bow.

5   Using one strand of **AL 303**, highlight with a few straight stitches on top of the ribbon.

6   Carefully cut the leaves out as close to the buttonholed edge as possible.

7   Whip stitch one bead of **2** closely around the edge of the leaf. Pick up and sew five beads of **2** along the centre vein and three beads of **2** to form the branches.

Beaded berries

Three beaded berries are positioned among the flowers.

1   Using two strands of **5** and a pebble bead, take the needle through and around the bead until it is fully covered with thread, leaving a tail of thread at the bottom to sew the berry in place on the slipper.

Cover pebble bead
with thread

Pick up two beads of **1** and cover the pebble bead.

Assemble the flowers on top of the slipper

1   Use a beading needle and thread to sew the flowers firmly in place.

2   Attach the thread to the bottom of each leaf and sew in place among the flowers.

3   Sew the berries in place using the tail of thread.

4   Sew the heart-shaped crystal to the top back of the slipper where the cord is attached.

Luxuriant leaves

Fanciful leaves are richly embroidered and beaded in this exuberant design that blends shape, colour and texture. Featured here on a decorative cushion, the design will add a touch of elegance to any home accessory.

WHAT YOU NEED

Pale mauve or aqua felt, 3 squares, each 20 cm × 20 cm (8" × 8")

Pale aqua dupion silk, 25 cm × 25 cm (10" × 10")

Pale mauve dupion silk, 25 cm × 25 cm (10" × 10")

Light-weight Shapewell (or Permashape), 25 cm × 25 cm (10" × 10")

24-gauge and 26-gauge beading wire

Approximate size of each leaf 17 cm × 14 cm (6¾" × 5½")

Threads

Kaalund Yarns 2-ply Wool	*Symbol*
1 skein 3211 (medium aqua)	**1**
1 skein 6480 (variegated aqua)	**2**

Kaalund Yarns Fine Wool	
1 skein 2402 (pale mauve)	**3**
1 skein 2430 (dark mulberry)	**4**
1 skein 2443 (medium mauve)	**5**

Kaalund Yarns Mulberry Silk	
1 skein S 132 (pale mauve)	**6**
1 skein S 84 (medium mulberry)	**7**
1 skein S 144 (variegated aqua)	**8**
1 skein S 131 (variegated mauve)	**9**

Kaalund Yarns Fine Mulberry Silk	
1 skein FS 144 (variegated aqua)	**10**

Kaalund Yarns Ambrosia	
1 skein wisteria	**11**

Kaalund Yarns Ripples	
1 skein wisteria	**12**

Kaalund Yarns Wispers	
1 skein wisteria	**13**

DMC Rayon Floss	
1 skein 30211 (light lavender)	**14**
1 skein 30504 (light blue-green)	**15**
1 skein 30550 (very dark violet)	**16**

Anchor Marlitt	
1 skein 857 (purple)	**17**

Needle Necessities Overdyed Floss

1 skein NNOD 194 (mauvelous)   **18**

Rajmahal Art Silk

1 skein 805 (sassafras)   **19**

Beads

Delica, size 11	*Symbol*
10 g DBR 923 (medium mauve)	**1**
10 g DBR 629 (light mauve)	**2**
3 g DBR 464 (dark purple)	**3**
10 g DBR 626 (aqua)	**4**
6 g DBR 502 (multicoloured silver)	**5**

Other beads

45 jade Czech lustre cut glass beads, 4 mm	**6**
60 amethyst Czech lustre cut glass beads, 4 mm	**7**
3 g dark amethyst bugle beads, size 1	**8**

STITCH SYMBOLS

A   stem stitch

AA whipped stem stitch

B   chain stitch

BB whipped chain stitch

C   close long buttonhole stitch

CC long and short buttonhole stitch

D   feather stitch

E   herringbone stitch

F   close fly stitch

G   small fly stitch

H   straight stitch

I   granitos stitch

J   French knot

K   detached chain stitch

L   short close buttonhole stitch

M   double knot stitch

N   laid stitch

O   long and short satin stitch

P   cross stitch

METHOD

Each leaf is embroidered and beaded separately. One strand of thread is used throughout unless otherwise indicated (Ripples and Wispers threads have only one strand). Work leaves 1 and 2 on the pale aqua silk and leaf 3 on the pale mauve silk.

1   Trace each leaf shape onto the right side of a separate piece of silk and mark the main lines of the design (see following pages for patterns). Work on one leaf at a time in the hoop.

2   Place a piece of light-weight Shapewell underneath the piece of silk and tack in place.

3   Using one strand of **8**, work a row of small running stitches around the outline of the leaf.

4   Embroider the leaf shape following the stitching diagram and referring to the stitch and thread symbols (see *What you need* for thread symbols).

5   Turn the work over in the hoop to the wrong side.

6   Cut a length of 26-gauge wire to fit around the leaf shape, allowing at little extra at each end. Starting at **X**, and using two strands of thread 18, couch the wire in place with small stab stitches, using the tacking stitch line as a guide.

7   Cut off excess wire.

8   You may find this step easier without a hoop. With the right side facing, work close short buttonhole stitch over the wire, changing threads and colours for the different sections of the edge (a–b, b–c and so on), as indicated on the stitching diagram

9   Work French knots along the bottom edge of the buttonhole stitch, following stitch and colour symbols.

10 Carefully cut the leaf out close to the buttonholed edge.

Leaf 1 pattern and stitching diagram

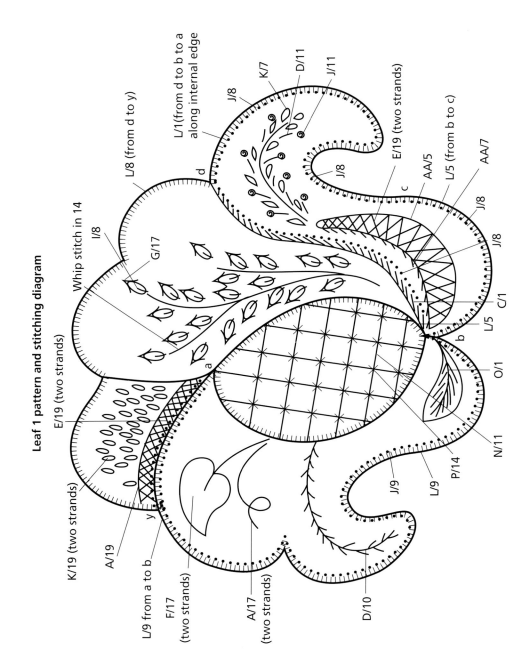

E/19 (two strands)

K/19 (two strands)

A/19

L/9 from a to b

F/17
(two strands)

A/17
(two strands)

D/10

Whip stitch in 14

L/8 (from d to y)

L/1(from d to b to a
along internal edge)

J/8

K/7

D/11

J/11

J/8

E/19 (two strands)

AA/5

L/5 (from b to c)

AA/7

J/8

J/8

C/1

L/5

O/1

N/11

P/14

L/9

J/9

I/8

G/17

a

b

c

d

y

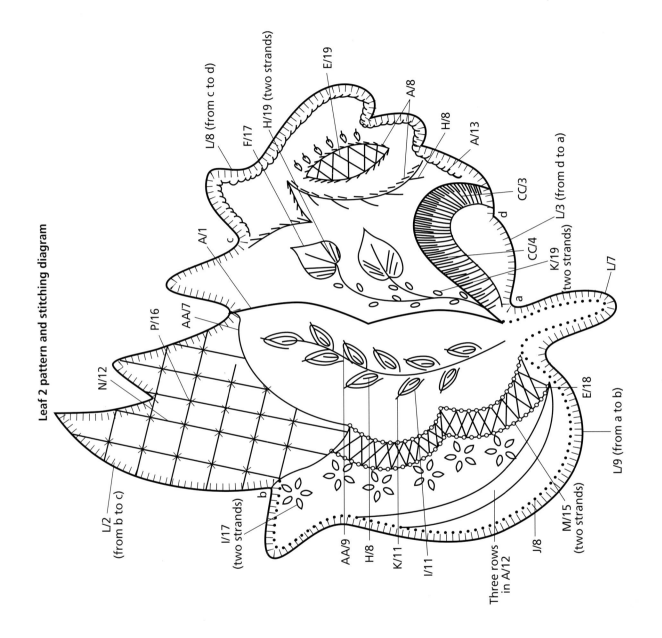

Leaf 2 pattern and stitching diagram

Luxuriant leaves

113

Leaf 3 pattern and stitching diagram

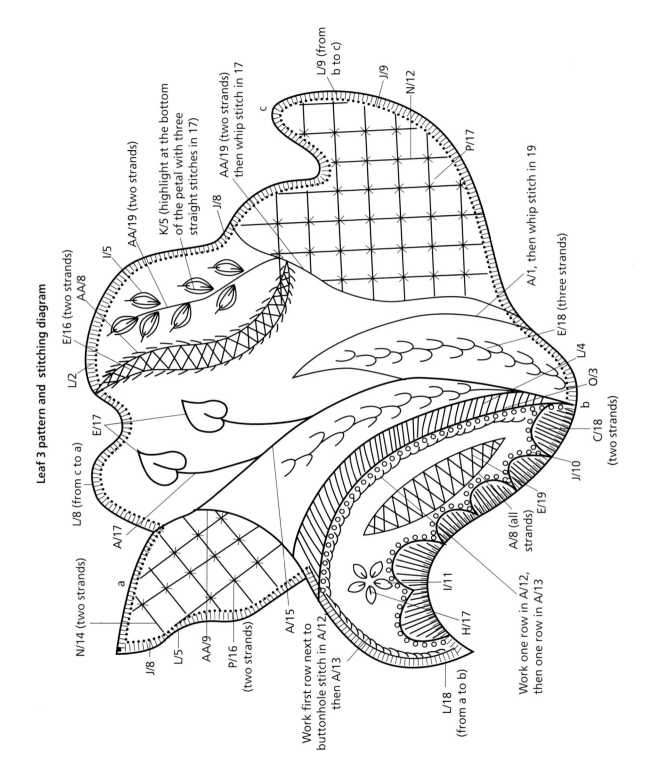

L/9 (from b to c)

J/9

N/12

P/17

A/1, then whip stitch in 19

E/18 (three strands)

L/4

O/3

C/18 (two strands)

J/10

E/19

A/8 (all strands)

Work one row in A/12, then one row in A/13

H/17

I/11

L/18 (from a to b)

A/15

Work first row next to buttonhole stitch in A/12, then A/13

P/16 (two strands)

AA/9

L/5

J/8

a

N/14 (two strands)

A/17

L/8 (from c to a)

E/17

L/2

AA/8

E/16 (two strands)

I/5

AA/19 (two strands)

K/5 (highlight at the bottom of the petal with three straight stitches in 17)

J/8

AA/19 (two strands) then whip stitch in 17

c

b

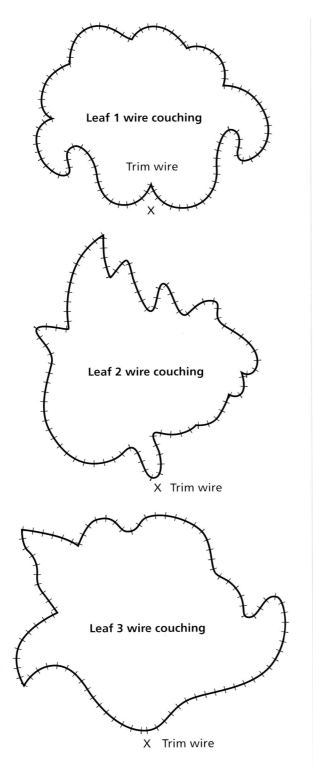

Leaf 1 wire couching

Trim wire

X

Leaf 2 wire couching

X Trim wire

Leaf 3 wire couching

X Trim wire

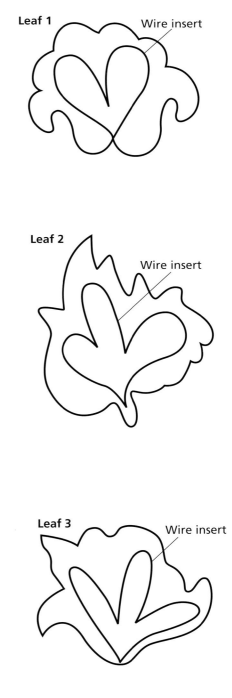

Leaf 1   Wire insert

Leaf 2

Wire insert

Leaf 3   Wire insert

11 Cut a length of 24-gauge wire to fit inside the leaf, bending as shown in the internal wiring diagrams.

12 Sandwich the loops of wire between the cut silk shape and a square of felt and tack roughly through all thicknesses to hold the wire in place (the tacking stitches are removed when the beading is complete).

13 Work the beading following the beading diagram and referring to bead symbols (see *What you need*).

14 Cut the leaf shape out of the felt, trimming the felt slightly smaller than the silk, and remove tacking stitches.

15 Place this piece right side up on another piece of felt that is about 2 mm (⅛") larger than the silk leaf and tack through all thicknesses to hold in place.

Leaf 1 beading diagram

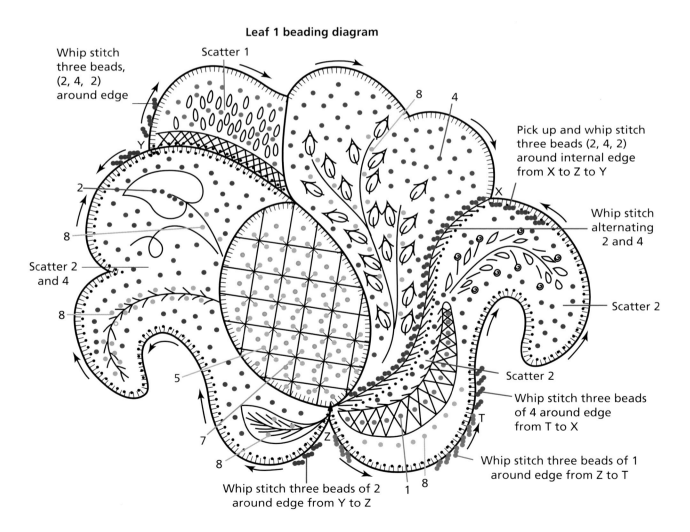

Whip stitch three beads, (2, 4, 2) around edge

Scatter 1

8

4

Pick up and whip stitch three beads (2, 4, 2) around internal edge from X to Z to Y

2

8

Scatter 2 and 4

8

Whip stitch alternating 2 and 4

X

Scatter 2

5

Scatter 2

7

Whip stitch three beads of 4 around edge from T to X

Z

T

8

1

8

Whip stitch three beads of 1 around edge from Z to T

Whip stitch three beads of 2 around edge from Y to Z

16 Referring to the beading diagram for colour, whip groups of three beads around the edge of the leaf, picking up the felt as well as the buttonholed edge (see *Techniques* for method).

17 Sew the leaves onto a purchased cushion or other background in an arrangement of your choice, bending them to create a three-dimensional effect and using slip stitches at the back to hold in place. If you decide to add some beads around the edge of the cushion as I have done, you will need more beads.

Leaf 2 beading diagram

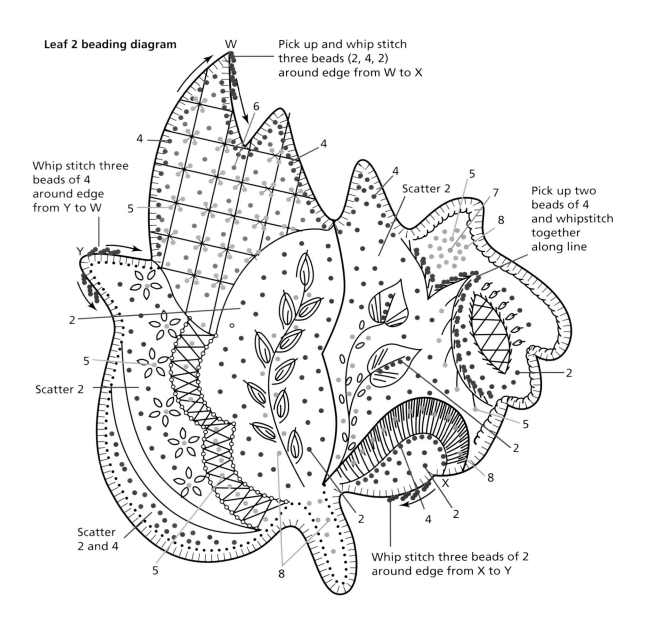

Pick up and whip stitch three beads (2, 4, 2) around edge from W to X

Whip stitch three beads of 4 around edge from Y to W

Scatter 2

Pick up two beads of 4 and whipstitch together along line

Scatter 2

Scatter 2 and 4

Whip stitch three beads of 2 around edge from X to Y

Leaf 3 beading diagram

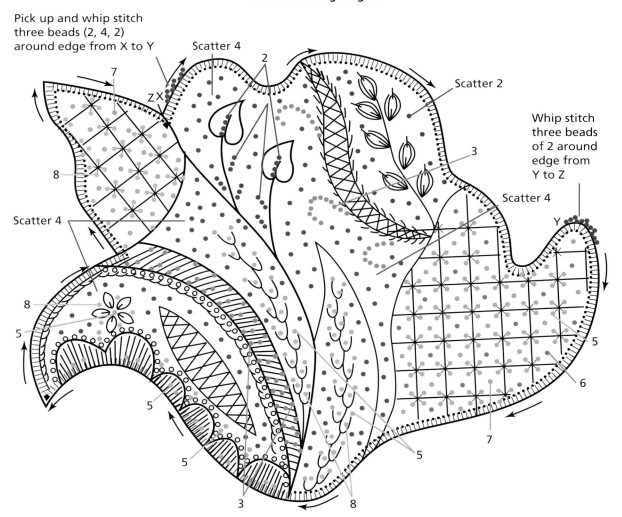

Pick up and whip stitch three beads (2, 4, 2) around edge from X to Y

Scatter 4

2

Scatter 2

Whip stitch three beads of 2 around edge from Y to Z

Scatter 4

Scatter 4

7

Z X

3

8

Y

8

5

5

5

5

5

5

6

7

3

8

Masquerade

Vivid blues and purples, exotic shapes and shimmering beads add to the excitement and air of mystery that this mask will lend to a 'masquerade' or any special occasion.

WHAT YOU NEED

Black silk satin, 40 cm × 140 cm wide (16" × 55")

Light-weight black Shapewell (Permashape), 25 cm × 115 cm wide (10" × 45")

Light-weight Pellon, 25 cm × 90 cm wide (10" × 36")

Soluweb, 25 cm × 90 cm wide (10" × 36")

Buckram, 20 cm × 90 cm wide (8" × 36")

Thick Vilene, 20 cm × 115 cm wide (8" × 45")

Black felt, 25 cm × 115 cm wide (10" × 45")

Black beading thread

24-gauge and 26-gauge beading wire

A stick about 33 cm (13") long

Finished size 22 cm × 25 cm (8½" × 10")

Threads

Colour Streams	Symbols
1 skein Silken Strands 14 (Monet)	**1**
1 skein Exotic Lights 21 (purple genie)	**2**

Anchor Marlitt	
858 (dark violet)	**3**
1067 (emerald green)	**4**
863 (plum pink)	**5**
836 (royal blue)	**15**
819 (purple)	**16**
1055 (light turquoise)	**17**

Anchor Stranded Cotton	
403 (black)	**6**

Anchor Lamé	
320 (bright blue)	**7**

Needle Necessities Overdyed Floss	
NNOD195 Coronation (purple)	**8**
NNOD 183 Jewels of the Nile (variegated purple and turquoise)	**9**

The Thread Gatherer Silk 'n Colors	
56 Mermaid Shimmer (turquoise)	**10**

Rainbow Gallery

Crystal Rays L166 (purple passion — purple and turquoise)	**11**

Rajmahal Art Silk

788 (perfect blue)	**12**

Cascade Yarns

Luminere 8055 (metallic blue and pinkish tones)	**13**

Kaalund Yarns

Woollie 2-ply Medium (pacific blue)	**14**

Beads
Delica, size 11

8 g DBC 29 (purple and gold)	**1**
3 g DBR 502 (silver multicoloured)	**2**
8 g DBR 10 (black)	**3**
2 g DBR 902 (pink)	**16**

Other beads

4 g gold bugle beads, size 1*	**4**
10 g two-cut turquoise, 2 mm**	
2 g blue-black sequins, 2 mm*	**6**
16 Bermuda blue round faceted crystals, 4 mm#	**7**
2 crystal heart drops, (1 purple, 1 vitrail), 10 mm#	**8**
16 vitrail crystal flowers, 5 mm#	**9**
5 yellow crystal flowers, 4 mm#	**10**
3 turquoise round faceted crystals, 5 mm#	**11**
3 purple iris glass faceted beads, 4 mm#	**12**
2 g bright green bugle beads, 2 mm*	**13**
1 medium vitrail round flat bead, 8 mm#	**14**
4 bright pink seed beads, size 10#	**15**
10 g two-cut black#	**17**

* Available from Creative Beadcraft
**Available from Photios Bros, item 646
\# Available from Bead Trimming and Craft

STITCH SYMBOLS

A	stem stitch
AA	whipped stem stitch
B	detached chain stitch
C	French knot
D	feather stitch
E	close feather stitch
F	granitos stitch (8 stitches unless stated otherwise)
G	long and short satin stitch
H	double knot stitch
I	close long buttonhole stitch
J	fly stitch
JJ	close fly stitch
K	laid stitch
L	cross stitch
O	straight stitch
P	spider stitch
Q	herringbone stitch

METHOD

The mask is made up of two separate pieces (front and back), which are joined together. The shapes are first embroidered and beaded, and then attached to the mask.

Mask base

1 Trace the mask pattern (see following page) onto the right side of the silk and tack a piece of light-weight Shapewell to the wrong side.

2 Using one strand of **6**, work a row of close small straight stitches around the outside and the eye openings.

Work small straight stitches around eye shapes and outside of mask

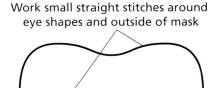

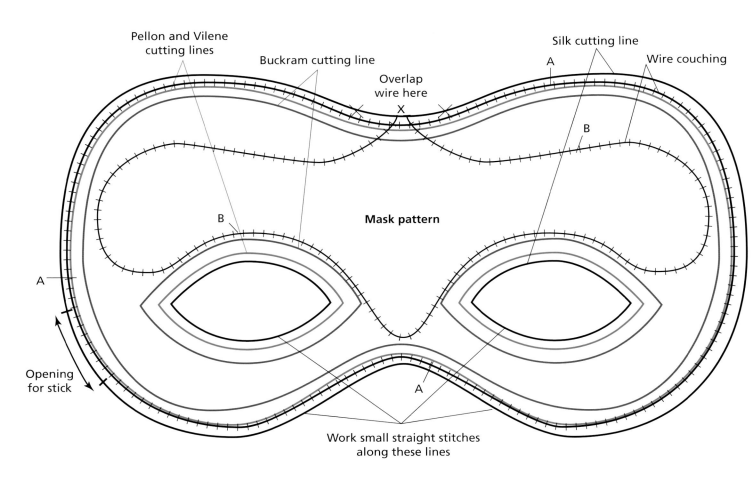

Pellon and Vilene cutting lines

Buckram cutting line

Overlap wire here

X

Silk cutting line

A

Wire couching

B

A

B

Mask pattern

A

A

Opening for stick

Work small straight stitches along these lines

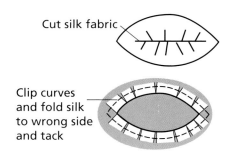

Cut silk fabric

Clip curves and fold silk to wrong side and tack

3 Work the surface beading of the mask following the bead symbols and the beading and positional diagram. Use small straight stitches to sew on the black sequins.

4 Cut the silk across the eye openings and very carefully trim the Shapewell back to the eye shape. Fold the silk to the wrong side, clip curves and tack close to the edges of the fold with small stitches. The silk will fray a little but the beading will cover this.

5 Trace the mask shape and eyes from the pattern sheet onto thick Vilene, marking wiring lines **A** and **B**.

6 Cut lengths of 24-gauge wire to fit around wiring line **A**, overlapping the ends of the wire at **X**. Cut another a length to fit around wiring line **B**, again overlapping the ends at **X**.

7 Couch the wire in place using two strands of cotton thread.

8 Cut a piece of Pellon following the Pellon cutting line on the mask pattern.

9 Cut a piece of buckram following the buckram cutting line on the mask pattern.

10 Repeat steps 1 to 9 to make the back of the mask, omitting the beading.

Beading and positional diagram

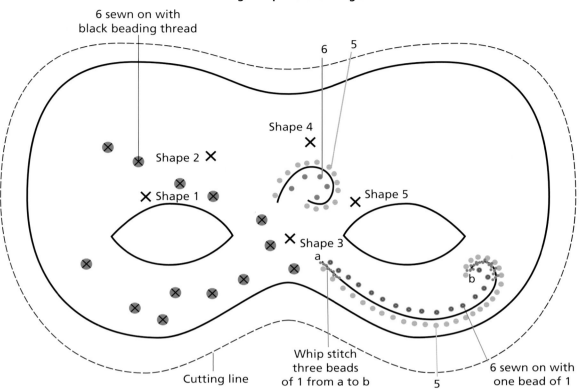

6 sewn on with
black beading thread

6   5

Shape 4
✕

Shape 2 ✕

✕ Shape 1

Shape 5

✕ Shape 3
a

Whip stitch
three beads
of 1 from a to b

Cutting line

5

b

6 sewn on with
one bead of 1

Assembling the mask base

1   Cut the beaded silk mask along the silk cutting line. Place on the Pellon and then on the wired Vilene, carefully matching up the eye openings (the Pellon and Vilene are slightly smaller than the silk), and tack in place.

2   Fold the silk over onto the back of the Vilene and over the wire, clipping curves, and tack close to the edges.

3   Repeat steps 1 and 2 with the unbeaded back of the mask.

4   Place the two pieces of buckram between the front and back silk pieces, lining up the eye openings and pin to hold in place. Whip stitch the two pieces together around the mask, leaving a small opening where indicated on the mask pattern to insert the stick.

5   Pick up and whip stitch three beads of **10** all around the outside of the mask and the eye openings, catching the edges of both silk mask pieces. At the stick opening, catch only the front of the mask.

Decorative shapes

There are five shapes, each of which is worked separately. Two strands of thread are used for embroidery unless stated otherwise. Repeat the following steps for each of the shapes.

1   Trace the shape and embroidery pattern onto a piece of soluweb so that it can be placed in a hoop. Place the soluweb on the right side of the silk. Place a piece of light-weight black Shapewell on the wrong side of the silk, pin in place and tack through all layers.

2   Using one strand of **9**, work a row of small straight stitches around the outside line.

3   Embroider, following the symbols for threads (see What you need) and stitches.

Shape 1

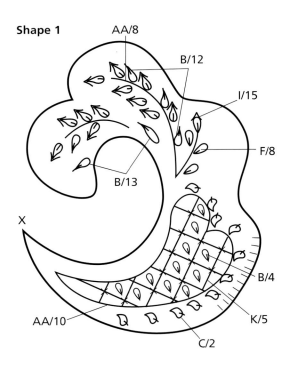

AA/8
B/12
I/15
F/8
B/13
X
AA/10
C/2
B/4
K/5

Shape 4

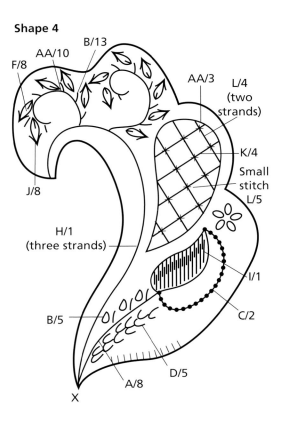

F/8
AA/10
B/13
AA/3
L/4 (two strands)
K/4
Small stitch
L/5
J/8
H/1 (three strands)
B/5
I/1
C/2
A/8
D/5
X

Shape 2

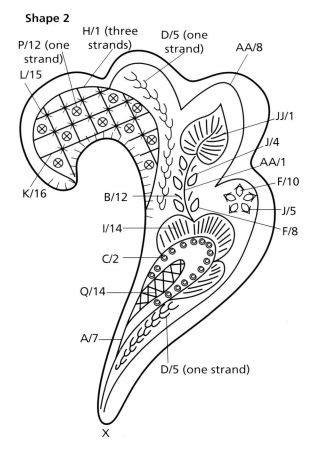

P/12 (one strand)
H/1 (three strands)
D/5 (one strand)
AA/8
L/15
JJ/1
J/4
AA/1
K/16
B/12
F/10
I/14
J/5
C/2
F/8
Q/14
A/7
D/5 (one strand)
X

Shape 5

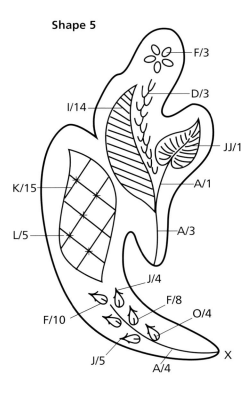

F/3
D/3
I/14
JJ/1
K/15
A/1
L/5
A/3
J/4
F/8
F/10
O/4
J/5
A/4
X

Shape 3

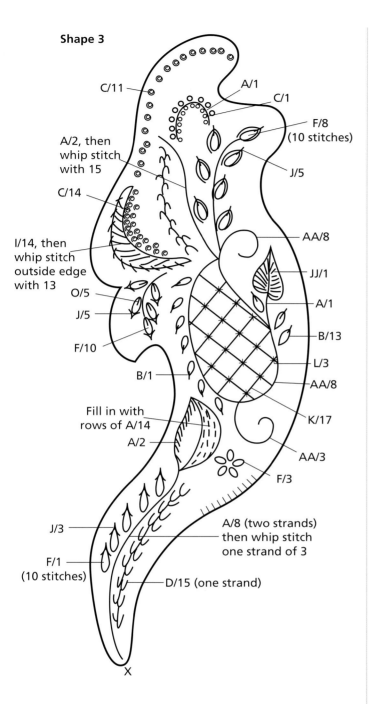

C/11

A/1

C/1

F/8
(10 stitches)

J/5

A/2, then
whip stitch
with 15

C/14

I/14, then
whip stitch
outside edge
with 13

O/5

J/5

F/10

B/1

Fill in with
rows of A/14

A/2

J/3

F/1
(10 stitches)

D/15 (one strand)

AA/8

JJ/1

A/1

B/13

L/3

AA/8

K/17

AA/3

F/3

A/8 (two strands)
then whip stitch
one strand of 3

X

4   Turn the work to the wrong side. Cut a length
of 26-gauge beading wire to fit around the
shape, overlapping the ends slightly at **X**, and
couch in place using two strands of **9**.

5   Turn work to the right side. Using three
strands of thread **6** and starting at **X**, work
close short buttonhole stitch over the wire.

6   Remove the work from the hoop and dissolve
the soluweb (see *Materials* for method).

7   Carefully cut the shape out as close as possible
to the buttonhole stitching and trim excess
wire.

8   Cut a piece of 24-gauge beading wire double
the length of the shape and fold in half.

9   Sandwich the wire between the embroidered
shape and a piece of felt. Tack with a few
stitches to hold the felt and embroidery
together while the beading is worked.

Wire inside shape

Wire inside
shape

125

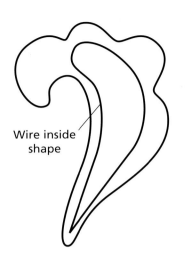

Wire inside shape

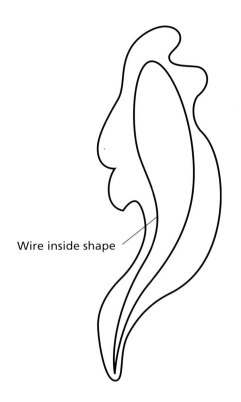

Wire inside shape

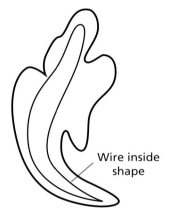

Wire inside shape

10 Place the shape back in the hoop and work the beading following the beading diagram and symbols (see *What you need*). Attach bead **17** at random over the embroidery.

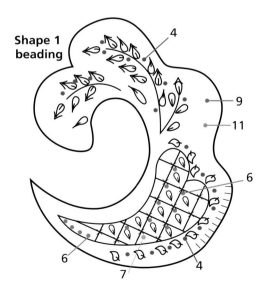

Shape 1 beading

4

9

11

6

6

7

4

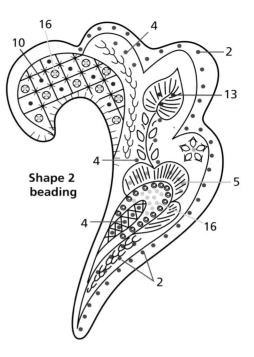

Shape 2 beading

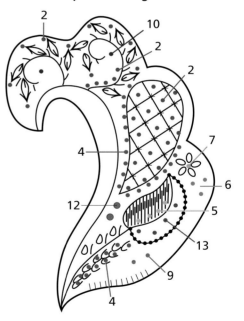

Shape 4 beading

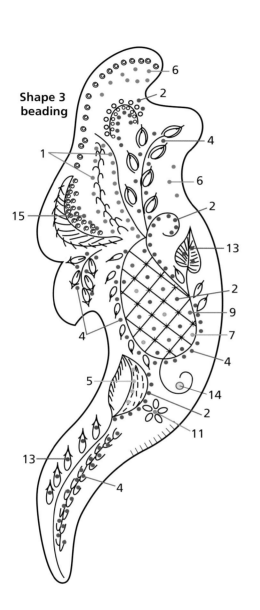

Shape 3 beading

Shape 5 beading

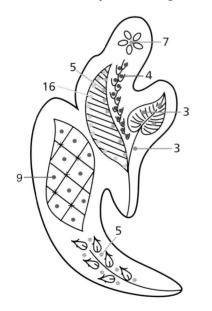

of one bead of **1**, one bead of **5**, one bead of **1** around the entire shape, catching the felt and just inside the buttonholed edge of the silk.

Assembling the mask

Secure beading thread to the bottom of shape 1 and, following the positioning diagram (see *Mask base*, step 3), sew the shape firmly in place through all thicknesses with stab stitches. Repeat with each shape.

The covered stick

1   Cut a length of silk to match the dimensions of the stick plus a small seam allowance. Fold in half lengthwise, right sides together, and machine a seam down the length of the silk and across one end. Turn to the right side and slip the stick inside the silk tube.

2   Place the raw end inside the opening left in the mask and slip stitch to secure.

3   Optional: scatter a selection of left-over beads over the stick.

11   Trim the felt back so that it is smaller than the silk. Pin the beaded shape carefully onto another piece of felt and trim the felt 2 mm (⅛") larger than the embroidered and beaded shape. Pick up and whip stitch combinations

Silken bands

Exquisite embroidery and light-catching crystals adorn these gently interwined silk bands to create an unusual accessory that will enhance any outfit or home décor. Worn separately, the connecting brooch becomes a unique piece of jewellery.

WHAT YOU NEED

Pale green silk satin (or colour of your choice), 50 cm × 140/150 cm (20" × 55/60")

Pale green dupion silk (or to match the silk satin), 50 cm × 115/90 cm (20" × 45/36")

Light-weight Shapewell (or Permashape), 40 cm × 115 cm (15½" × 45")

Green felt, 30 cm × 115 cm (12" × 45")

Pellon, 8 cm × 90 cm (3¼" × 36")

4.5 m (4½ yd) number 6 piping cord

24-gauge and 26-gauge beading wire

Dental floss

Ring clasp for necklace

Wooden brooch, diameter 5 cm (2")

Small piece of stiff cardboard for brooch back

Gold-coloured brooch pin

Finished size 40 cm long × 6 cm wide (15½" × 2½")

Threads

The Caron Collection	Symbols
1 skein Waterlilies 101 (cherry)	**1**

The Thread Gatherer Silk 'n Colors	
1 skein 023 (frosted auburn)	**2**

Kaalund Yarns	
1 skein Indulgence, sundown	**3**
1 skein Ripples, sundown	**4**
1 skein Skink, sundown	**5**
1 skein Skink, forest floor	**6**
1 skein Woollie 2-ply Medium, rose pink	**7**

Anchor Stranded Cotton	
1 skein 260 (pale green) or to match your choice of dupion silk	**8**

Anchor Marlitt	
1 skein 1209 (dark terracotta)	**9**

Beads

Delica, size 11   *Symbols*

8 g DBR 461 (antique copper)**	**5**
6 g DBR 685 (silver-lined dark rose)**	**6**
4 g DBR 671 (satin olive)**	**7**

Other beads

9 dozen padparadcha (dark apricot) crystal bicones, 3 mm*	**1**
7 ruby crystal bicones, 4 mm*	**2**
50 dorado (gun metal) round faceted crystals, 4 mm*	**3**
30 g olive lustre cut glass beads, 4 mm**	**4**
6 g bronze two-cut bugle beads, 2 mm*	**8**
6 g dark pink satin seed beads*	**9**
6 smoke topaz round faceted crystals, 5 mm*	**10**

STITCH SYMBOLS

A stem stitch
AA whipped stem stitch
C French knot
D feather stitch
E detached chain stitch
F cast-on stitch (16 per petal)
G straight stitch
H fly stitch
HH close fly stitch
I granitos stitch (8 stitches)
J long and short satin stitch
K laid stitch
L herringbone stitch
M close long and short buttonhole stitch
MM close short buttonhole stitch
N cross stitch
O Indulgence couched with one strand of 1
P close long buttonhole stitch
Q chain stitch
R double knot stitch
S pistil stitch

*Available from Bead Trimming and Craft
**Available from Maria George

METHOD

These intertwined bands of silk can be worn as a necklace or used as a curtain tie-back. Without the brooch they can be used to trim a collar or the neckline of a top.

The bands

The necklace consists of four silk bands, each embroidered and beaded in a different way. The following steps apply to each band.

1 Trace the outline and main embroidery lines onto the right side of the silk satin and tack a piece of Shapewell underneath the silk.

2 Work small running stitches along the outer pattern line.

3 Work the embroidery and beading following the embroidery and beading diagrams, and referring to symbols (see *Stitch symbols* and *What you need*). Use the two-needle method to work the cast-on stitches (see *Stitch glossary*). Do not sew the smoke topaz beads (**10**) in the centre of the F/1 flowers at this stage.

4 Cut out the band approximately 1.5 cm (½") larger than the pattern to allow for the seam.

5 Fold the seam allowance to the wrong side, clipping curves and using the small tacking stitches as a guide. Tack again close to the folded edge.

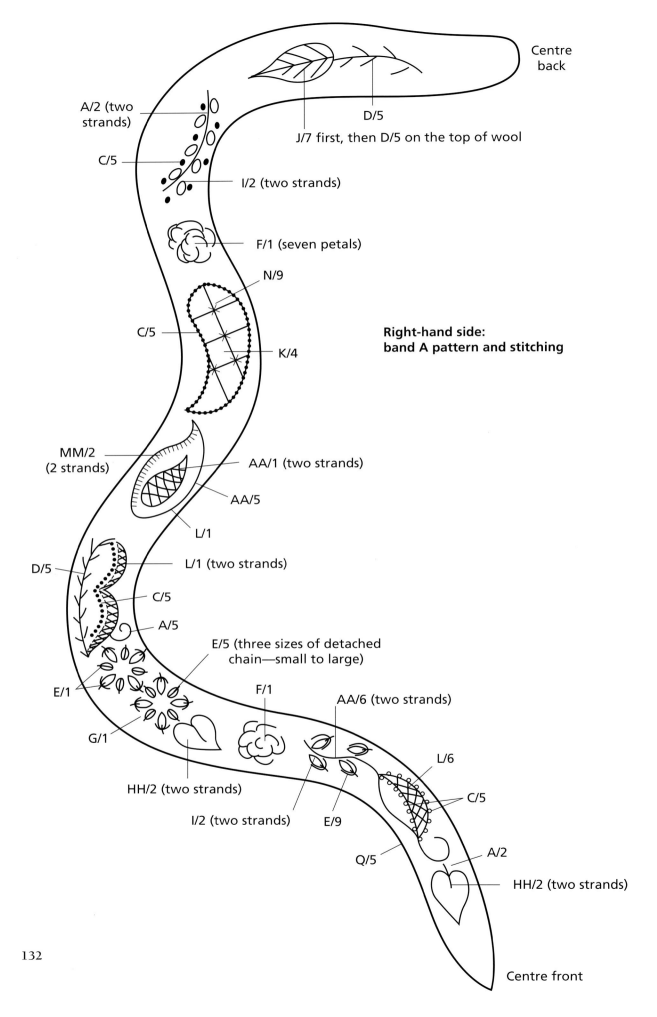

Centre back

A/2 (two strands)

C/5

I/2 (two strands)

J/7 first, then D/5 on the top of wool

D/5

F/1 (seven petals)

N/9

C/5

K/4

**Right-hand side:
band A pattern and stitching**

MM/2
(2 strands)

AA/1 (two strands)

AA/5

L/1

D/5

L/1 (two strands)

C/5

A/5

E/5 (three sizes of detached
chain—small to large)

F/1

AA/6 (two strands)

L/6

E/1

C/5

G/1

HH/2 (two strands)

I/2 (two strands)

E/9

Q/5

A/2

HH/2 (two strands)

Centre front

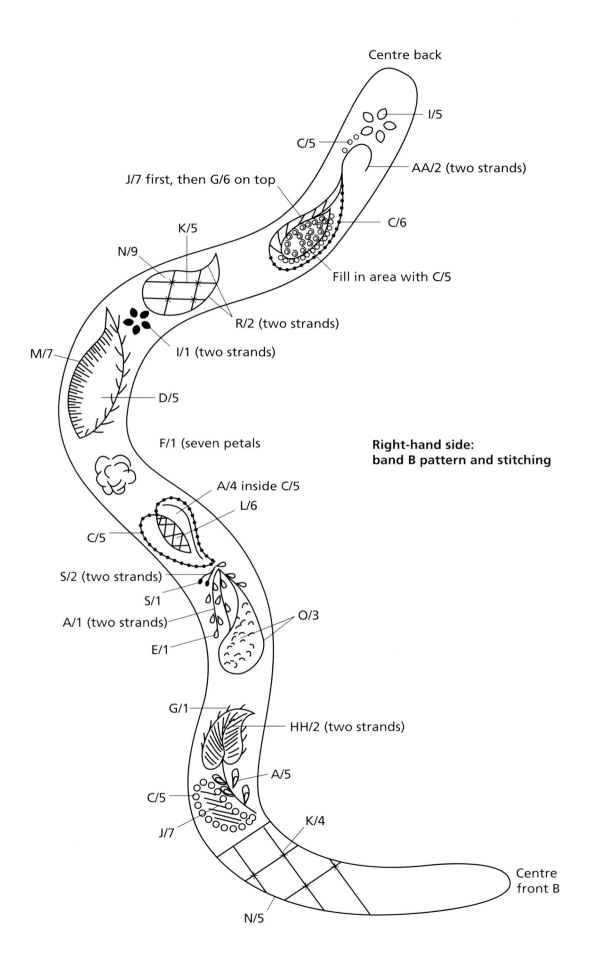

Centre back

I/5

C/5

AA/2 (two strands)

J/7 first, then G/6 on top

C/6

K/5

Fill in area with C/5

N/9

R/2 (two strands)

I/1 (two strands)

M/7

D/5

F/1 (seven petals

**Right-hand side:
band B pattern and stitching**

A/4 inside C/5

L/6

C/5

S/2 (two strands)

S/1

A/1 (two strands)

E/1

O/3

G/1

HH/2 (two strands)

A/5

C/5

K/4

J/7

Centre
front B

N/5

133

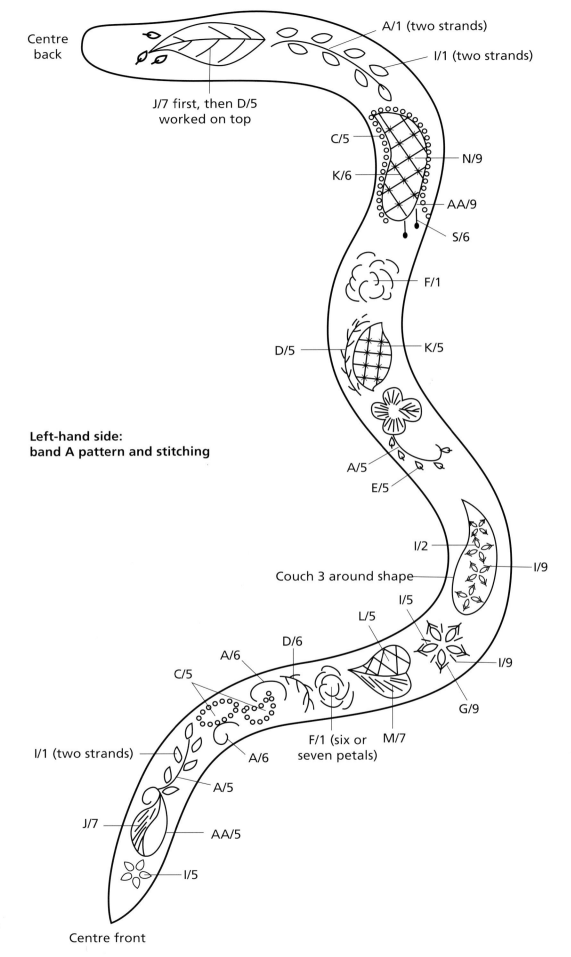

Centre back

J/7 first, then D/5 worked on top

A/1 (two strands)

I/1 (two strands)

C/5

N/9

K/6

AA/9

S/6

F/1

D/5

K/5

Left-hand side: band A pattern and stitching

A/5

E/5

I/2

I/9

Couch 3 around shape

I/5

L/5

I/9

D/6

G/9

A/6

C/5

M/7

F/1 (six or seven petals)

I/1 (two strands)

A/6

A/5

J/7

AA/5

I/5

Centre front

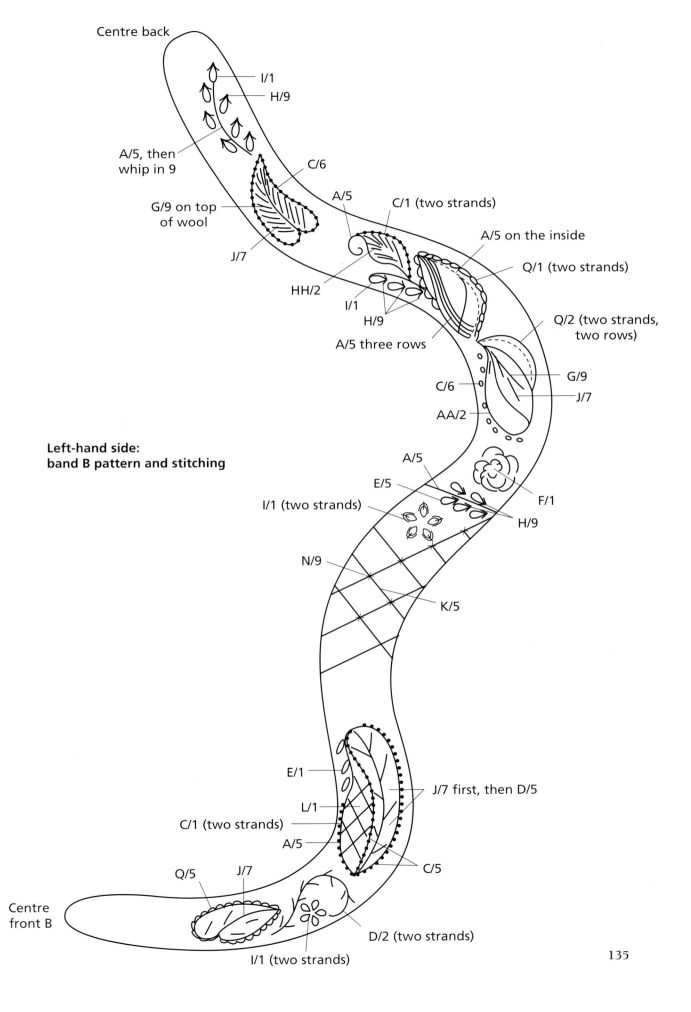

Centre back

I/1

H/9

A/5, then
whip in 9

C/6

G/9 on top
of wool

J/7

A/5

C/1 (two strands)

A/5 on the inside

Q/1 (two strands)

HH/2

I/1

H/9

A/5 three rows

Q/2 (two strands,
two rows)

C/6

G/9

J/7

AA/2

**Left-hand side:
band B pattern and stitching**

A/5

E/5

I/1 (two strands)

F/1

H/9

N/9

K/5

E/1

J/7 first, then D/5

L/1

C/1 (two strands)

A/5

C/5

Q/5

J/7

Centre
front B

D/2 (two strands)

I/1 (two strands)

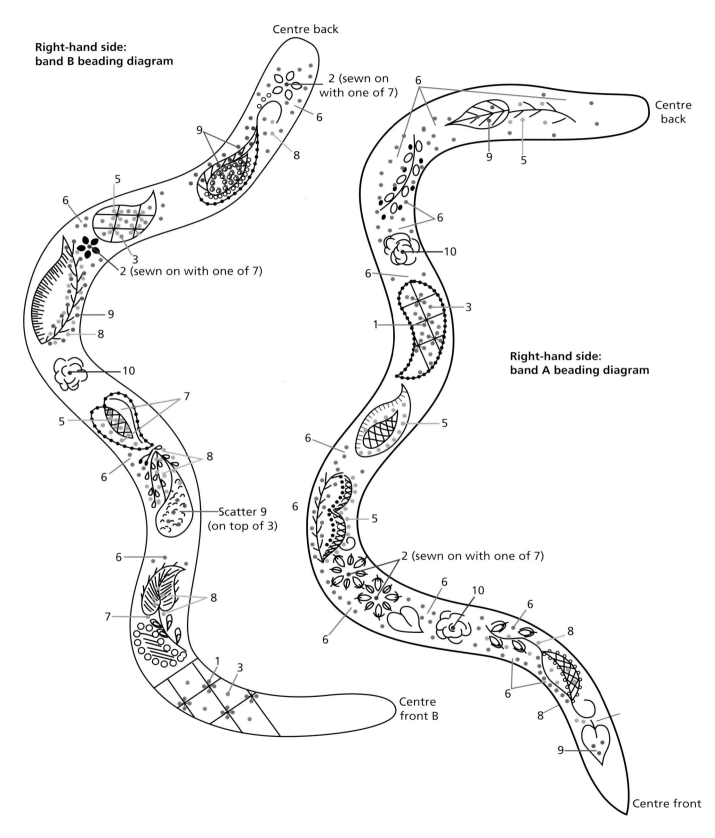

Centre back

**Right-hand side:
band B beading diagram**

2 (sewn on
with one of 7)

6

9

8

5

6

3

2 (sewn on with one of 7)

9

8

10

7

5

6

8

Scatter 9
(on top of 3)

6

8

7

1   3

6

Centre back

6

Centre
back

9   5

6

10

6

1   3

**Right-hand side:
band A beading diagram**

5

6

5

6

5

2 (sewn on with one of 7)

6   10

6

6

8

6   6

8

9

6

Centre
front B

Centre front

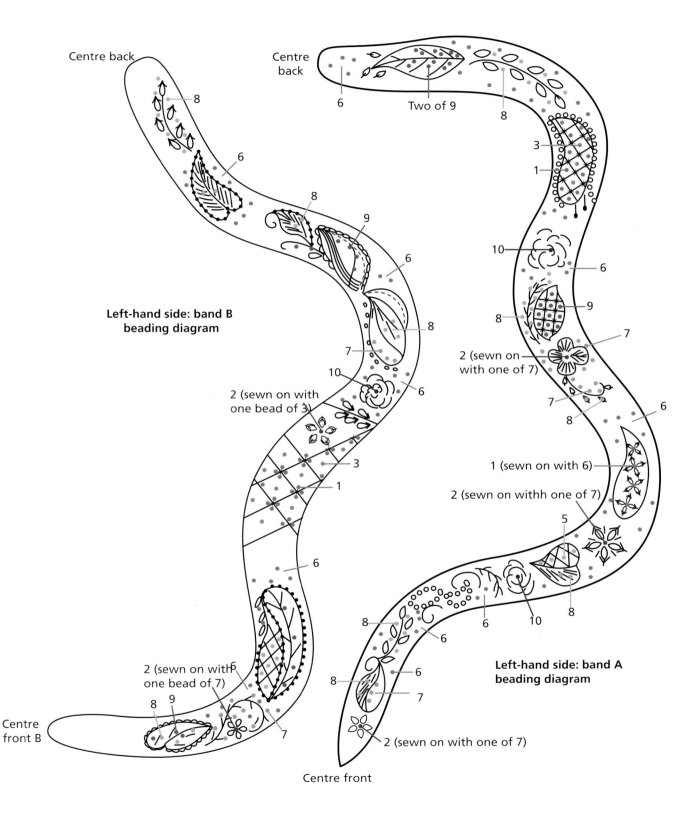

Centre back

8

Centre back

6

Two of 9

8

3

1

10

6

9

8

7

7

8

6

1 (sewn on with 6)

2 (sewn on withh one of 7)

5

8

6

10

8

6

6

Left-hand side: band A beading diagram

8

6

7

8

6

7

2 (sewn on with one of 7)

Centre front

6

Left-hand side: band B beading diagram

8

9

6

8

7

10

2 (sewn on with one bead of 3)

3

1

6

6

2 (sewn on with one bead of 7)

8

9

7

Centre front B

To finish each band

1   Cut a piece of dupion silk on the bias 2.5 cm (1") longer than the length of the band and 5 cm (2") wider.

2   Cut a piece of piping cord the length of the embroidered band, and another piece 10 cm (4") shorter. Place the two lengths of piping cord side by side so that the longer cord protrudes 5 cm (2") at each end. This will make the front and back ends of the band taper slightly, allowing them to sit flat at the back of the neck and at the centre front.

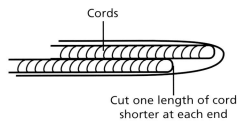

Cords

Cut one length of cord shorter at each end

3   Fold the silk lengthwise, wrong sides together, over the two cords, matching the raw edges. With small running stitches, sew a seam close to the cords along the full length so that the seam sits along the centre.

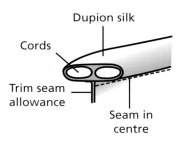

Dupion silk

Cords

Trim seam allowance

Seam in centre

Assembling the bands

1   Place the right-hand bands **A** and **B** together with tops matching and intertwine them so that the flowers are facing outwards, away from the neck, stretching the bands to elongate them as you go. Stitch together with slip stitches at the top and bottom to hold in place.

2   Sew one bead of **10** firmly in the centre of the flowers, taking the beading needle through all layers. This holds the intertwined bands together.

4   Trim the seam to 5 mm (⅜"). Place the covered cords with the seam along the centre against the wrong side of the embroidered silk band, and pin to hold in place.

5   Wrap the edges of the embroidered band over onto the covered cords and slip stitch along both sides. This makes the band slightly rounded.

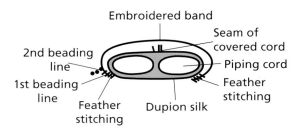

Embroidered band

Seam of covered cord

2nd beading line

Piping cord

1st beading line

Feather stitching

Feather stitching

Dupion silk

6   Using two strands of **8**, work feather stitch over the slip stitching to neaten.

7   Fold the silk under at each end and neaten.

8   Pick up one bead of **5** and one of **7** together and whip stitch this combination along the edges and ends of the band (not on the feather stitching). Then pick up one bead of **8**, one of **4** and one of **8** together and whip stitch along the edges and ends just behind the first combination.

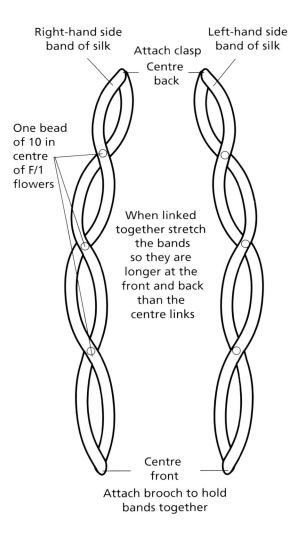

Right-hand side band of silk

Attach clasp

Left-hand side band of silk

Centre back

One bead of 10 in centre of F/1 flowers

When linked together stretch the bands so they are longer at the front and back than the centre links

Centre front

Attach brooch to hold bands together

139

3   At the back of the bands pull the intertwined sections together by picking up a combination of three beads of **8** as shown.

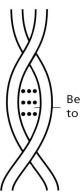

Beading with three beads of 8 to pull bands together slightly

4   Repeat steps 1–3 with bands **A** and **B** for the left-hand side.

5   Attach the clasp to the bands at the back of the neck.

Brooch

To make the brooch, two pieces of silk are embroidered and beaded, and then attached to a covered wooded brooch.

1   Trace brooch patterns **A** and **B** and the outlines of the embroidery onto the right side of the silk fabric. Tack a piece of Shapewell to the wrong side.

Brooch A pattern

Brooch B Pattern

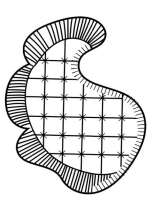

Brooch A stitching

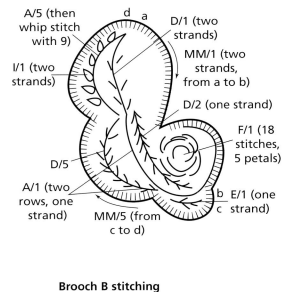

A/5 (then whip stitch with 9)

I/1 (two strands)

d   a   D/1 (two strands)

MM/1 (two strands, from a to b)

D/2 (one strand)

F/1 (18 stitches, 5 petals)

D/5

A/1 (two rows, one strand)

MM/5 (from c to d)

b   E/1 (one c strand)

Brooch B stitching

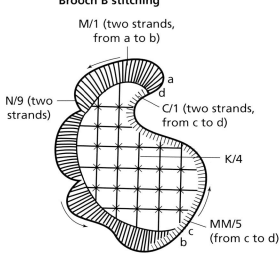

M/1 (two strands, from a to b)

N/9 (two strands)

a
d

C/1 (two strands, from c to d)

K/4

MM/5 (from c to d)

c
b

2   Using thread **8**, sew a small running stitch along the outer pattern line.

3   Work the embroidery following the stitch diagrams, and referring to the symbols (see *Stitch symbols* and *What you need*).

4   Turn the work over. Cut a length of 26-gauge wire to fit around each shape, overlapping the wires slightly at **X**. Using two strands of **8**, couch the wire around the edge.

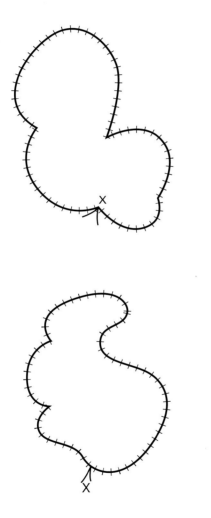

5   Turn the work back to the right side. Work either close short buttonhole stitch or close long buttonhole stitch around the edge over the wire, using the thread and stitches indicated by the symbols on the stitching diagram.

6   Carefully cut each piece out close to the buttonholed edge and trim excess wire.

7   Cut a piece of 24-gauge wire the length of each embroidered shape. Sandwich the wire between a piece of felt and the wrong side of each embroidered shape and pin to hold.

8   Following the beading diagram and bead symbols (see *What you need*), work the beading on the right side of the embroidered shapes.

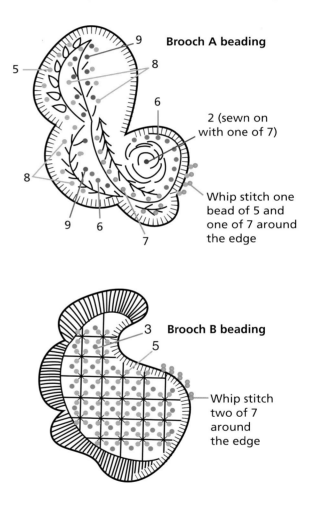

9   Trim the felt slightly smaller than the silk.

10 Cut additional pieces of felt slightly larger than the worked shapes and pin to hold in place.

11 Pick up one bead of **5** and one of **7** and whip stitch around the edge, catching the felt and the buttonhole stitch.

Brooch assembly

1 Cut a piece of stiff cardboard for the back of the brooch the same size as the wooden brooch front.

2 Cut two pieces of silk satin fabric 1.5 cm (½") larger all round than the brooch front.

3 Cut two pieces of Pellon the same size as the front and back of the brooch.

4 Using dental floss, sew a row of running stitches close to the edge of one piece of silk. Place a piece of Pellon in the centre of the fabric, then the wooden brooch on top, and pull up the gathering stitches. Lace the back on the wrong side and pull it firmly into shape.

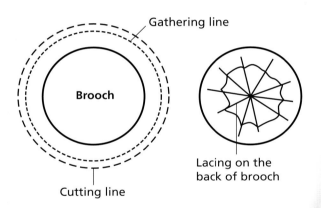

Gathering line

Brooch

Cutting line

Lacing on the back of brooch

5 Repeat step 4 for the back of the brooch.

6 Using a matching thread, attach a brooch pin to the back of the brooch a short way down from the top edge. Place the wrong sides of the brooch front and back together. Pick up one bead of **5** and one of **7** and whip stitch this combination around the edge of the brooch, catching both the front and back sections.

7 Using a beading needle and thread and following the photograph for position, attach brooch shapes A and B to the front of the brooch, catching the felt at the back of each shape and the silk of the brooch.

Completing the necklace, tie-back or trim

1 To use as a necklace or a curtain tie-back, pin the two intertwined bands together with the brooch at the front.

2 If using as a trim for a collar or a top, attach the bands to the garment with a few stitches at the centre back of collar, then about half-way down the collar and then at the front. When working the beading, sew some extra crystals at the bottom and top ends of the band to fill, as no brooch will be used.

Christmas stocking

*This magnificent Christmas stocking –
decorated with Christmas balls, holly and berries
– promises to contain an equally exciting gift for
someone special and will be a wonderful addition
to your festive decorations for years to come.*

WHAT YOU NEED

Pattern sheet B

Dark cream dupion silk, 50 cm × 115 cm
  (20" × 45")

Light-weight Pellon, 50 cm × 90 cm
  (20" × 36")

Light-weight Shapewell (or Permashape),
  50 cm × 115 cm (20" × 45")

Vilene, 15 cm × 30 cm (6" × 12")

30-gauge green covered wire

*Finished size 19 cm wide × 30 cm long
  (7½" × 12")*

Threads

Colour Streams

10 metres Silk Ribbon 30 (eucalypt), 4 mm

2 skeins Silken Strands (SS) 30 (eucalypt)

Anchor Stranded Cotton (ASC)

1 skein 70 (burgundy)

1 skein 683 (green)

Anchor Lamé (AL)

1 skein 303 (gold)

Beads

Delica, size 11	*Symbol*
3 g DBR 42 (silver-lined gold)	**1**
10 g DBC 27 (metallic green)	**2**
6 g DBC 29 (purple and gold mix)	**3**
8 g DBR 31 (bright gold)	**4**
8 g DBR 105 (burgundy)	**5**

Other beads	
30 g Siam (red) crystals, 4 mm*	**6**
9 gold bicone crystals, 4 mm	**7**
10 g two-cut red beads, 2 mm approx.	**8**
6 g gold bugle bead, 2 mm	**9**
8 purple iris cut (faceted) glass, 4 mm*	**10**
12 Rosemonte AB crystals in claws, 4 or 5 mm**	**11**
12 Mill Hill small red pebble beads (for berries)	

*Available from Maria George

** Available from Bead Trimming and Craft

METHOD

The stocking is first quilted and then decorated with five Christmas balls, sprigs of holly and berries. A beaded cuff, silk lining and beaded tab complete the stocking.

1   Trace the stocking pattern from the large pattern sheet B onto the right side of the cream dupion silk, including the quilting lines. Tack a piece of Shapewell underneath the silk.

2   Using one strand of **AL 303**, quilt along the quilting lines, except for the Christmas balls.

Christmas balls

1   Bead Christmas balls A–E, starting with A, following the beading diagrams and referring to the bead symbols (see *What you need*).

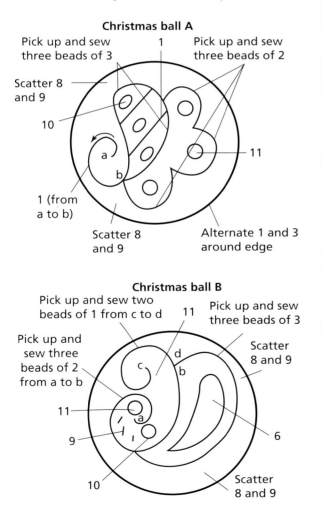

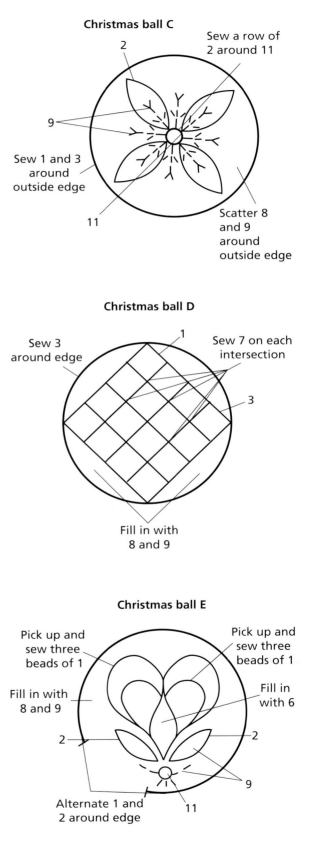

145

2 When all the beading on the balls is complete, bead their strings. Sew a line of # **4** beads first, not too close together, along each string. Pick up three beads of **3** and backstitch through each # **4** bead, changing your thread from side to side so that the beads sit alternately to the left and right of the string.

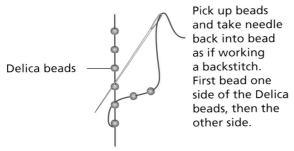

Delica beads

Pick up beads and take needle back into bead as if working a backstitch. First bead one side of the Delica beads, then the other side.

Note: this diagram is enlarged. The Delica beads should be closer together.

Cuffs

The cuff consists of two flaps, each beaded differently. The small flap is placed on top of the larger one, matching the top right-hand corners.

Small flap

1 Trace the design onto the right side of the dupion silk and tack a piece of Shapewell underneath. Work the beading following the beading diagram and referring to the symbols.

2 Cut out beaded flap along the cutting line and place right sides together onto another piece of silk, but do not cut out.

3 Sew along the lines marked, leaving an opening at the top. Cut off the excess fabric and clip the seam. Turn inside out and whip stitch the opening closed.

Small flap of cuff

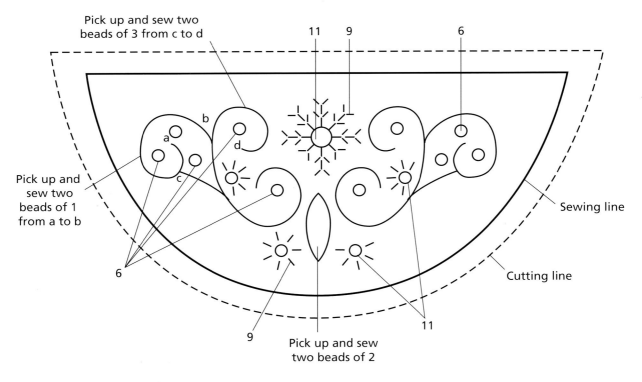

Pick up and sew two beads of 3 from c to d

11   9   6

Pick up and sew two beads of 1 from a to b

6

Sewing line

Cutting line

9

Pick up and sew two beads of 2

11

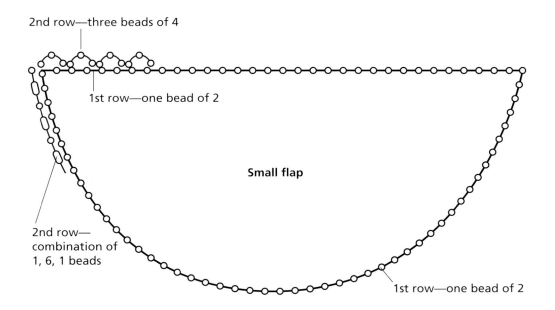

2nd row—three beads of 4

1st row—one bead of 2

Small flap

2nd row—
combination of
1, 6, 1 beads

1st row—one bead of 2

4 Whip stitch one bead of **2** all the way round the edge. Along the top straight edge behind this row, pick up and whip stitch three beads of **4**. Around the curved edge behind the first row of beads, whip stitch a combination of one bead of **1**, one bead of **6**, one bead of **1**.

Large flap

1 Repeat steps 1–3 as for the small flap, but following the pattern and beading diagram for the large flap.

2 Whip stitch one bead of **2** around the part of curve that will be visible. Behind the first row of beads, whip stitch a combination of one bead of **1**, one bead of **6**, one bead of **1**.

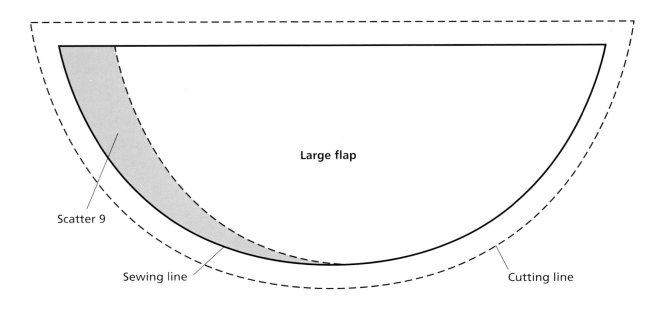

Large flap

Scatter 9

Sewing line

Cutting line

Holly leaves

There are five small holly leaves, twelve medium-sized leaves, and three large leaves. The following steps apply to all the leaves.

1 Trace the holly leaf pattern onto Vilene. Cut a length of 30-gauge wire to fit around the leaf, overlapping the wire slightly at **X**.

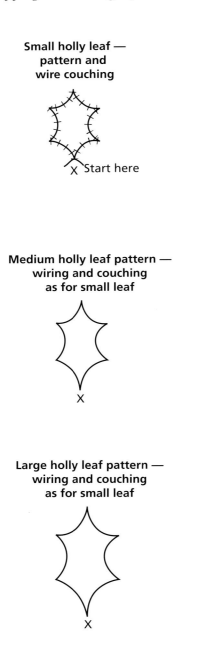

**Small holly leaf —
pattern and
wire couching**

X Start here

**Medium holly leaf pattern —
wiring and couching
as for small leaf**

X

**Large holly leaf pattern —
wiring and couching
as for small leaf**

X

2 Couch the wire around the edge using two strands of **ASC 683**.

3 Using three strands of **SS 30**, work close short buttonhole stitch over wire, bringing each stitch up a needle's width outside the wire.

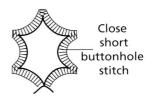

Close
short
buttonhole
stitch

4 Using the silk ribbon, embroider long and short satin stitch around the edge, bringing the needle up between the wire and the buttonhole stitch. Fill the remainder of the holly leaf with the ribbon in long and short satin stitch.

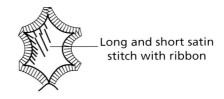

Long and short satin
stitch with ribbon

5 With one strand of **AL 303**, highlight the leaf with a few straight stitches on top of the ribbon, fanning out from the centre.

6 Pick up and stitch approximately five beads of **2** along the centre vein of the holly leaf, and three beads of **2** along the branches.

Two beads of 2 around outside

Five beads of 2 along centre vein

Three beads of 2 along branches

X

7   Carefully cut the leaf out. If any white Vilene is visible, touch up around the edges with a green marker. Trim excess wire.

8   Whip stitch two beads of **2** all around the leaf.

Berries

Work 12 berries. Cover red pebble beads with two strands of **ASC 70** and burgundy beads (**5**), following the method used for the berries in the Splendid slipper project.

149

Assembling the leaves and berries

The positions of the smaller leaves are marked on the stocking pattern sheet with **X**. The positions of the medium leaves are marked with **XX**.

1   Attach a length of **ASC 683** to the bottom of each leaf. Place the leaf with right side facing the front of the stocking and stitch firmly in place. Bend the leaf back so that the right side shows.

2   Attach the berries to the top of each group of holly leaves.

Assembling the stocking

1   Cut out the beaded stocking.

2   To make the back of the stocking, tack a piece of Pellon to the wrong side of a piece of silk larger than the stocking front.

3   Place the beaded stocking onto the plain silk, right sides together, and tack in place. Sew around the stocking along the seam line, leaving the top open. Trim excess fabric and clip curves.

4   Cut out another two stocking shapes from pattern sheet B for the lining. Place right sides together and sew the seam, leaving an opening at the top and side of the stocking, as indicated on the pattern.

5   With right sides together, slip the lining inside the stocking and stitch around the top, leaving a small opening at the top right hand side to insert the beaded tab. Pull the front of the stocking carefully through the side opening of the lining and slip stitch the side opening closed. Push lining neatly down inside the stocking.

6   Starting at the top of the stocking, whip stitch one bead of **2** around the sides and bottom of the stocking, but not around the top.

7   Behind this row, whip stitch a combination of one bead of **1**, one bead of **6**, one bead of **1**.

Cuffs

1   Pin the larger flap to the top edge of the stocking and tack in place. Whip stitch with two beads of **2** around the top edge, attaching the cuff as you go.

2   Place the small flap on top of the large flap and attach with small slip stitches close to the top edge of the stocking. Pick up three beads of **4** and whip stitch across the top left edge of the small flap so that the beading continues the row already sewn along the top edge of the large flap.

Beaded tab

1   Cut a piece of silk 18 cm × 4 cm (7" × 1½"). Fold in the raw edges lengthwise from the sides to the centre.

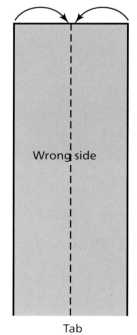

Fold edges in

Wrong side

Tab

2 Approximately 5 mm (¼") in from one of the long folded edges, sew one bead of **6**, then three beads of **9** sewn singly, then another bead of **6**, and repeat all along the edge up to approximately 1.5 cm (½") from the end.

3 Fold the length of silk in half lengthwise to cover the stitching.

4 Whip stitch two beads of **2** along the long edge, catching the two folded edges together to form the tab. Repeat along the other folded edge.

5 Fold in half to form a loop, placing raw edges together at the bottom and neaten. Insert the raw edges into the tab opening at the top of the stocking and sew securely.

6 Attach the three large holly leaves and three berries at the base of the tab.

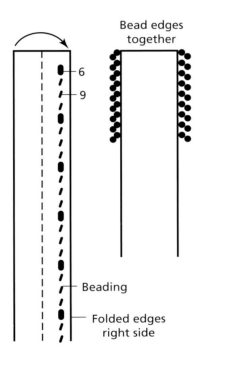

Old-fashioned Santa

This Santa is not a weekend project but a labour of love for your family to enjoy and hand down to generations to come. The dimensional work on the robe was inspired by seventeenth-century embroidery from England, while the beads add sparkle and glitter to a unique ornament for a special time of year.

WHAT YOU NEED

Pattern sheets C, D, E and F

Rich red silk satin, 50 cm × 140/150 cm (20" × 55/60")

Pale coffee silk satin, 40 cm × 140/150 cm (16" × 55/60")

Red satin lining, 30 cm × 115/90 cm (12" × 45/36")

Coffee-coloured cotton or bemsilk lining, 30 cm × 115 cm (12" × 45")

1 m (1 yd) light-weight wadding, 1 cm (⅜") thick

1 m (1 yd) Pellon

Light-weight black Shapewell (Permashape), 60 cm × 90 cm (24" × 36")

2 m (2 yd) stiff black net

Scraps of soft black tulle

1.5 m (1.5 yd) burgundy or plum-coloured fake fur, pre-cut to 8 cm (3¼") wide (or, if not pre-cut, 30 cm/12" × width)

Burgundy felt, 20 cm × 115 cm (8" × 45") or three 20 cm (8") squares

24-gauge and 26-gauge beading wire

30-gauge green covered wire

Dental floss

Large handful mohair for Santa's beard

Porcelain Santa head and hands (from Lyn Spencer), or make from moulds

For the stand: Craft wood 1 cm (⅜") thick, 15 cm x 15 cm (6" x 6") with a 1 cm (⅜") hole drilled in the centre ; 43 cm (17") length of 12 mm (½") dowel; wire coat hanger

Finished height approximately 51 cm (20")

Threads

Anchor   *Symbols*

1 skein Marlitt 843 (Christmas red) **AM 843**

3 skeins Stranded Cotton 1005
   (burgundy)   **ASC 1005**

1 reel Ophir 300 (gold)   **AO 300**

1 skein Lamé 303 (gold)   **AL 303**

The Thread Gatherer Silk 'n Colors

1 skein 054 (tapestry green)   **SNC 054**

Beads

Delica

10 g DBR 29 (metallic medium
   bronze iris), size 11 *   **1**

15g DBR 34 (light gold). size 11 *   **2**

10 g DBC 27 (metallic teal iris), size 11 * **3**

30 g DBL 42 (gold), size 8*   **4**

Other beads

71 AB Rosemonte beads
   (CRO197-SS17AB), 4.5 mm**   **5**

100 Siam (red) glass pearls, 6 mm***   **6**

Gold bugle beads, size 1[#]   **7**

8 round topaz AB 5 mm crystals (5301)*   **8**

12 Siam (red) crystals, 5 mm
   (sold in string)*   **9**

10 g two-cut red beads,
   2 mm approx.[##]   **10**

*Available from Maria George
**Available from Bead Trimming & Craft
***If not available from Bead Trimming & Craft, Maria George will dye burgundy to order. Alternatively use Gutermann Glasperlen 773891 (burgundy), 6 mm.
[#] Available from Creative Beadcraft
[##] Available from Photios Bros, item 315

METHOD

The old-fashioned Santa consists of:

- a stand and a body, with purchased face and hands

- a pale coffee-coloured silk satin skirt with a beaded front and a plain back

- a quilted and beaded overskirt in red silk with two beaded dimensional shapes attached to each of the curved front edges

- a red silk bodice

- quilted and beaded sleeves with cuffs formed by beaded dimensional shapes

- a quilted and beaded hat with a beaded dimensional shape attached to it.

To make the stand and body

1   Screw the dowel firmly into the base from underneath.

2   Drill a hole through the dowel 6.5 cm (2½") from the top.

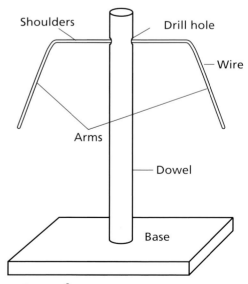

Drill 1 cm ($\frac{3}{8}$") hole and screw the dowel in from underneath with countersunk screw

3 Cut the hook off the wire coat hanger, straighten out the wire and cut a length of 53 cm (21"). Pass the wire through the hole in the dowel and bend to form Santa's shoulders and arms (length from shoulders to end of arms 16.5 cm/6½").

4 Cut three strips of Pellon, each 5 cm x 50 cm (2" x 20"). Wrap one strip in a figure of eight around the dowel and the wire where they meet.

5 To form Santa's arms, attach the other two Pellon strips to the wire on either side of the dowel (Santa's neck). Wrap each around the wire tightly down to the end and then back up to the dowel, securing with dental floss. Wrap the whole of each arm entirely with dental floss and secure.

6 Fold the black net into three so that it reaches from under the arms to the bottom of the stand.

7 Using the dental floss, sew a row of running stitches along the top edge. Pull up tightly to gather and secure at the back, but do not trim the excess floss.

8 Attach the net around the stand by taking the dental floss over and under each shoulder and through the net from back to front a couple of times, forming braces to hold the net in place.

9 To shape the waist, run a line of gathering stiches around the net 8 cm (3") down from the arms, pull up the stitches and then wrap the floss around the net to draw it in.

10 Place the stand to one side until the garment pieces are complete and you are ready to assemble Santa.

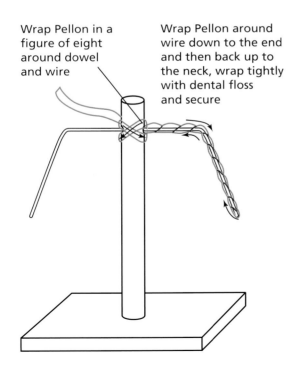

Wrap Pellon in a figure of eight around dowel and wire

Wrap Pellon around wire down to the end and then back up to the neck, wrap tightly with dental floss and secure

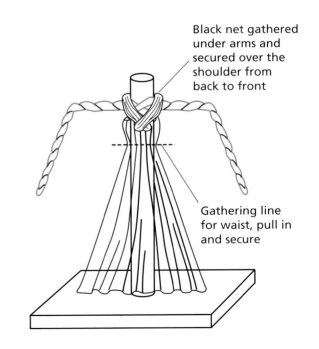

Black net gathered under arms and secured over the shoulder from back to front

Gathering line for waist, pull in and secure

Santa's skirt

1 Trace the design from pattern sheet C onto a piece of coffee-coloured silk satin.

2 Tack a piece of light-weight Shapewell onto the wrong side of the silk satin.

3 Secure beading thread to match the silk at one end of one of the scrolled lines. Pick up a combination of one bead of **3**, one bead of **2**, one bead of **3** and, taking the needle forward the size of one bead, pick up a small amount of silk from right to left across the line, then pull the beads onto the line. Working the beading close together in this way makes the beads stand up slightly so that they resemble cording.

4 Continue in this way around the entire scroll. When you have almost reached the end of a scroll, decrease the beading by picking up one of **3** and one of **2** together twice, and then one of **2** once. This tapers the ends of the scrolls to a sharper point.

5 Pick up one bead of **2** and sew in rows along all the quilting lines of the middle front section of the skirt.

6 Tack a piece of Pellon to the wrong side of the beaded silk and quilt the grid in one strand of **AM 843**.

7 Secure thread at **A** in the top centre square (see pattern sheet C). Pick up one bead of **3**, one of **6**, one bead of **3**, and take the needle back through the silk at virtually the same spot. Repeat this for each square on the centre front of the skirt.

8 At all positions marked **X**, form the berries as follows. Secure beading thread at **X**, pick up one bead of **3**, one of **6**, three beads of **3**, take

the needle back through the pearl and the top **#3** bead and through the fabric. Secure in place. Repeat twice more in the same position. Behind each group of berries, pick up twelve beads of **3** and take the needle back through almost the same hole to form a loop at the back of the berries, and repeat.

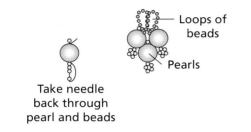

Take needle back through pearl and beads

Loops of beads

Pearls

9 Cut the beaded skirt front out. Using pattern sheet C, cut one from the coffee-coloured silk satin for the back of the skirt and two from the lining fabric. With right sides together, join the back and front silk pieces at the side seams. Repeat with the lining pieces. With right sides together and matching side seams, sew the lining to the skirt along the bottom edge. Clip the seam and turn to the right side, bringing the lining up through the skirt to the top. Neaten around the top of the skirt.

10 Measure a length of fur to fit around the bottom front edge of the skirt. Fold in half lengthwise and whip stitch in place. Taper the fur at each side seam by folding under slightly.

Red overskirt

1 Trace pattern sheet D onto a piece of red silk satin but do not cut out.

2 Tack the wadding to the wrong side of the silk. Using **AO 300**, quilt along all lines.

3 On the bold lines, bead over the quilting with **#2** beads sewn close together.

4 Sew a small gold bugle bead (**7**) on either side and all along the remaining quilted lines on alternate sides, as shown on the pattern.

5 Cut out the overskirt and place right sides together on top of the plain red lining (but do not cut the lining out). Tack around all edges, then machine around sides and bottom of overskirt, leaving the top curved section open. Turn to the right side.

6 For the band of the overskirt; cut a length of red silk satin 39 cm x 6.5 cm (15½" x 2½"). With right sides together, sew the band to the overskirt. Fold the band over to the wrong side, fold the raw edge under and slip stitch along the length of band (finished depth of band 2 cm/¾").

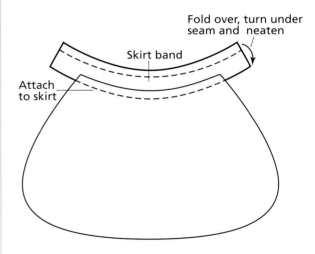

Fold over, turn under seam and neaten

Skirt band

Attach to skirt

7 Whip stitch one bead of **4** along the bottom edge of the skirt from **X** to **X**.

8 Whip stitch one bead of **4** along the top edge of the band and along the seam line where it is attached to the skirt.

9 Work the beaded dimensional shapes (see below) and attach them to the overskirt with a few slip stitches just under the front edge to hold them securely in place.

10 Attach a press stud to the skirt band and sew the medium-sized holly leaves (see page 161) to the centre front. Sew the berries on as for the coffee silk skirt (step 8).

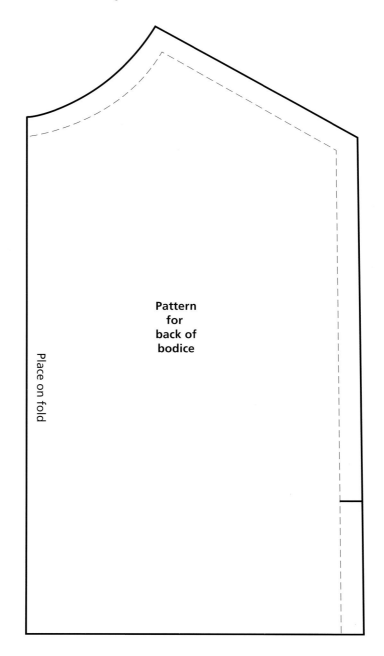

Pattern for back of bodice

Place on fold

Bodice

1   Cut out front and back bodice patterns from the red silk satin, wadding and lining.

2   Join the lining pieces at the shoulder seams. Tack the silk pieces to the wadding, then place right sides together and join the front to the back at the shoulder seams.

3   Place the lining and the silk right sides together. Starting at the bottom of one front edge, sew up the front edge, around the neck and down the other front edge. Clip and trim the seam. Turn to the right side and press.

4   Turn under the raw armhole edges and slip stitch to neaten.

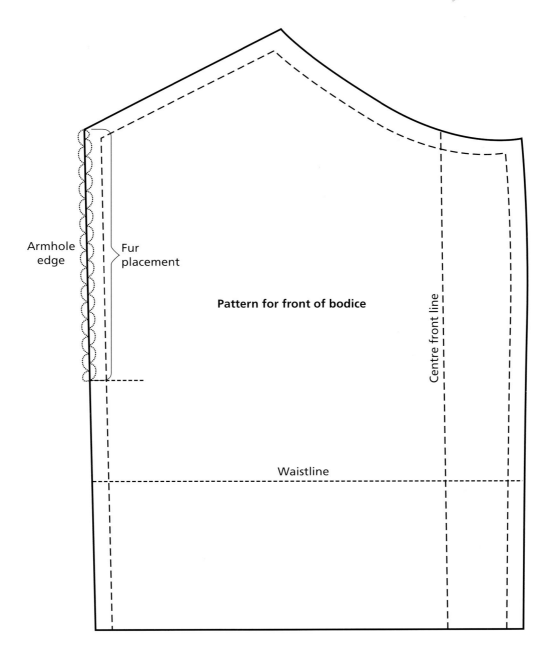

Pattern for front of bodice

Armhole edge

Fur placement

Centre front line

Waistline

5   Cut two pieces of fur each 21 cm x 7 cm wide (8¼" x 2¾"). Fold in half lengthwise. Place right side of fur to right side of silk and whip stitch in place as marked along one armhole edge. Repeat this step for the second armhole edge.

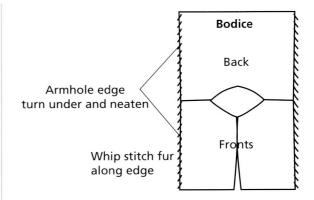

Bodice

Back

Armhole edge
turn under and neaten

Whip stitch fur
along edge

Fronts

6   Sew a few beads of **4** at random on the back of the bodice.

7   Whip stitch one bead of **4** down one of the front edges from the neck to the waistline.

Sleeve

1   Using pattern sheet E, trace the sleeve and quilting design onto the red silk satin.

2   Tack a piece of wadding onto the wrong side of the silk. Using **AO 300**, quilt along all lines.

3   On the bold lines, bead over the quilting with **#2** beads sewn close together.

4   Sew a small gold bugle bead (**7**) all along and on either side of the remaining quilted lines, as shown on the pattern.

5   Cut out the quilted silk sleeve piece. Cut out the sleeve from the lining fabric. Place right sides of the sleeve and lining together, sew along the bottom edge and open out.

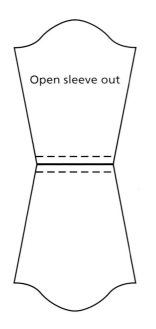

6   Fold the sleeve in half lengthwise, wrong sides together, and sew along the full length of the lining and silk seams.

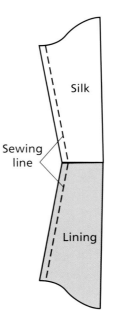

7   Pull the lining through to the inside of the silk, then turn inside out.

8   Cut a length of fur 3.5 cm (1⅜") wide to fit around the finished cuff of the sleeve. Fold the fur in half lengthwise and, with the right side of the fur to the beaded side of the sleeve, whip stitch the fur around the bottom edge of the sleeve, then fold the fur back to the right side of the sleeve.

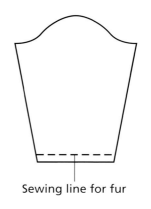

9   Turn the sleeve to the right side and neaten the top through all thicknesses.

10 Make the second sleeve in the same way.

Hat

1   Using pattern sheet F, repeat steps 1–4 as for the sleeves.

2   Cut out the quilted hat shape. Cut out the hat pattern from the red lining fabric.

3   Fold the beaded silk piece and the lining piece in half lengthwise and sew each separately along the seam line.

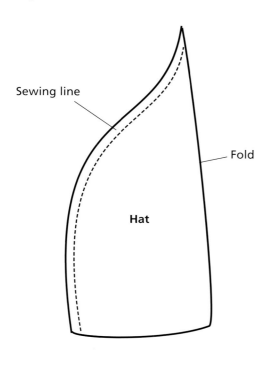

Sewing line

Fold

Hat

4   Place the lining inside the beaded silk hat, wrong sides together and matching seams. Turn the bottom edges under and slip stitch together to neaten.

5   Cut a length of 8 cm (3¼") wide fur to fit around the bottom of the hat and fold in half lengthwise. Place the right side of the fur to the wrong side of the hat and whip stitch in place. Fold the fur back to the right side of the hat. This gives a good finish around Santa's face.

6   Sew three large holly leaves (see page 164) together and make the berries as in step 8 for the coffee silk skirt. Attach the leaves and berries to the fur on one side of the hat at the front.

7   Attach the beaded dimensional shape (see below) to the front of the hat where the fur turns back.

8   Make a tassel for the point of Santa's hat with a mixture of beads.

Beaded dimensional shapes

Two different shapes (A and B) are attached to the front edges of the overskirt. These are are worked in reverse for the opposite side of the overskirt. The cuffs of the sleeves are formed by two dimensional shapes (shape C), one of which is worked in reverse. The shape on the front of the hat is the same as the sleeve shape (shape C). The following steps are worked for each shape.

1   Trace the shape and beading design onto the right side of the red silk satin.

2   Tack a piece of light-weight Shapewell onto the wrong side of the silk.

3   Work a row of small stitches around the outside line of each shape.

4   Bead the shape following the beading symbol chart, but do not attach any of the Rosemonte crystals (**5**), gold Delica beads (**4**) or crystals (**8** and **9**) at this stage.

5   Cut a piece of 26-gauge wire to fit around the shape. Starting at **X** on the wrong side and using two strands of **ASC 1005**, couch the wire in place using the tacking line as a guide.

6   Turn the work back to the right side and work close short buttonhole stitch in the same thread around the shape over the wire. Cut the shape out as close to the buttonholed edge as possible and trim excess wire.

7   Measure a piece of 24-gauge wire to fit inside the shape, as shown in the diagrams.

Shape A pattern and beading

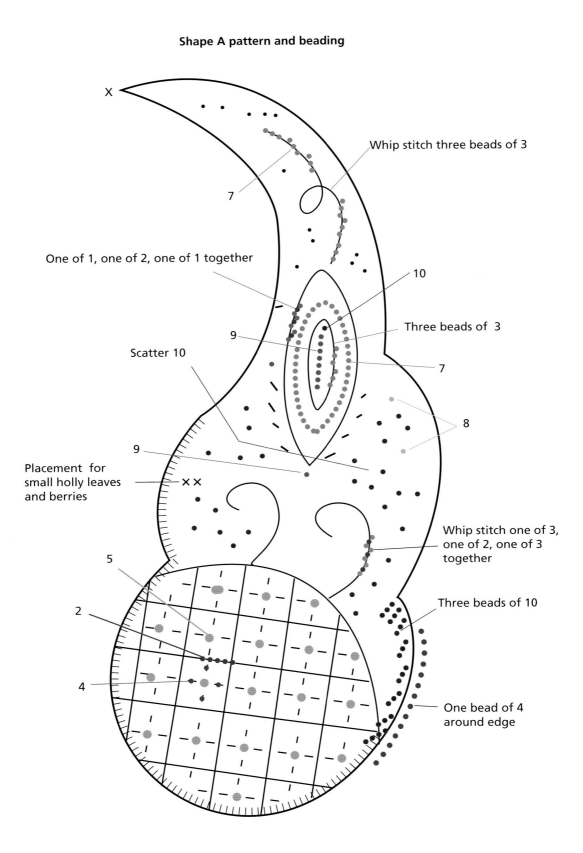

X

Whip stitch three beads of 3

7

One of 1, one of 2, one of 1 together

10

Three beads of 3

9

7

Scatter 10

8

9

Placement for
small holly leaves
and berries

× ×

Whip stitch one of 3,
one of 2, one of 3
together

5

Three beads of 10

2

4

One bead of 4
around edge

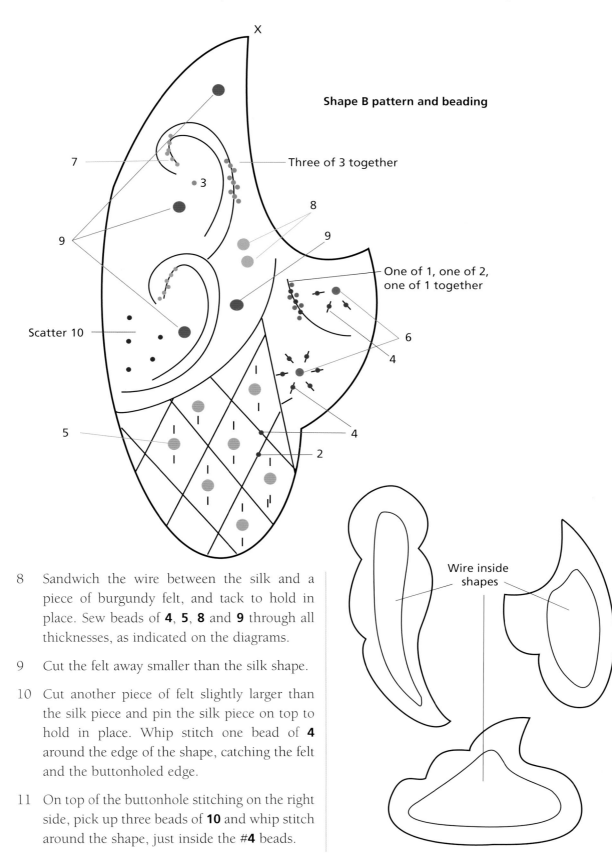

Shape B pattern and beading

Three of 3 together

7

3

8

9

9

One of 1, one of 2,
one of 1 together

6

Scatter 10

4

4

5

2

4

Wire inside
shapes

8   Sandwich the wire between the silk and a piece of burgundy felt, and tack to hold in place. Sew beads of **4**, **5**, **8** and **9** through all thicknesses, as indicated on the diagrams.

9   Cut the felt away smaller than the silk shape.

10   Cut another piece of felt slightly larger than the silk piece and pin the silk piece on top to hold in place. Whip stitch one bead of **4** around the edge of the shape, catching the felt and the buttonholed edge.

11   On top of the buttonhole stitching on the right side, pick up three beads of **10** and whip stitch around the shape, just inside the #**4** beads.

Shape C pattern and beading
(for second cuff, work one in reverse)

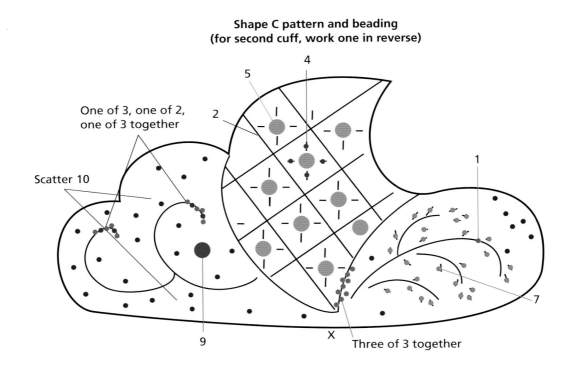

12 Attach small holly leaves at **XX** on the lower skirt shape and work three berries as in step 8 for the coffee skirt.

Holly leaves

There are three large, five medium and six small leaves. Each is worked in the same way.

1 Trace the three holly leaf patterns onto Vilene.

2 Cut a length of green covered wire to fit around each leaf shape, crossing the ends at **X**.

3 Using two strands of **SNC 054**, couch the wire around the shapes on the right side, working extra stitches at the points and bending the wire with either small pliers or eyebrow tweezers.

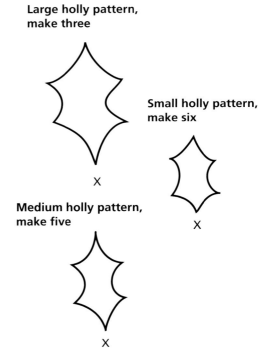

Large holly pattern, make three

Small holly pattern, make six

Medium holly pattern, make five

Wire couching

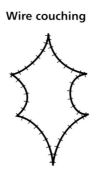

Beading

X

4   Using two strands of **SNC 054**, work long and short buttonhole stitch around the shapes over the wire. Fill in the shapes with long and short satin stitch in **SNC 054**.

Stitch direction

5   Using one strand of **AL 303**, work straight stitches at random on the top of the silk to highlight.

Highlighting

6   Carefully cut around each of the holly leaves and trim excess wire.

7   Pick up two beads of **3** and bead around the leaves. Pick up four or five beads of **3** and sew on the leaf to form veins.

8   Sew the leaves in position on the skirt band, hat or dimensional shape.

Santa's head and hands

1   Using a hot glue gun, attach the mohair around Santa's face in sections to form a beard. (I use a metal teaspoon to press the mohair in place to avoid burning my fingers.)

2   Glue small pieces of mohair on the face for eyebrows and a moustache.

3   Glue a small amount of mohair on the head at the front and around the back near the neck.

4   Place a small amount of glue inside the hands and quickly push the ends of the wire arms inside the hands.

5   Place a small amount of glue on top of the head and attach the hat securely.

Assembling Santa

1   Place the coffee silk skirt over the top of the stand to fit around the waist.

2   Starting at the shoulder and using dental floss, sew a row of gathering stitches around the top of the sleeve.

3   Slip the sleeve over the wire arm and place a small quantity of fine tulle inside the sleeve.

4   Pull the dental floss up around top of sleeve and attach to the top of the shoulder.

5 Repeat with the other sleeve.

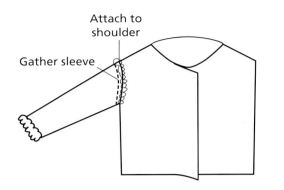

6 Place the bodice over the top of the dowel and tuck inside the skirt, overlapping the centre front edges. You may need to overlap the centre front more at the waistline than at the neck.

7 Catch the side seams of the bodice together from the underarms to the waist with a few small stitches.

8 Wrap a small amount of Pellon around the top of the dowel and sew to hold in place. Place Santa's head over the top of the dowel and pull the one side of the front bodice over the other to hold his head in place and secure with slip stitches.

9 Fold under the raw edges of the coffee silk skirt at the waist and slip stitch in place to the bodice.

10 Place the beaded red overskirt around Santa's waist.

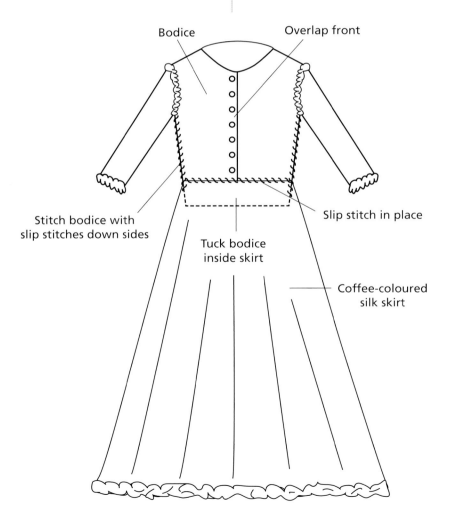

Stitch glossary

Close feather stitch

Cast-on stitch worked with two needles

Chain stitch

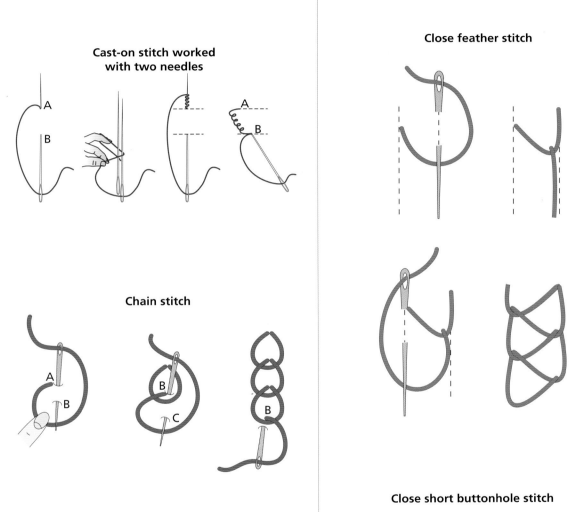

Close short buttonhole stitch

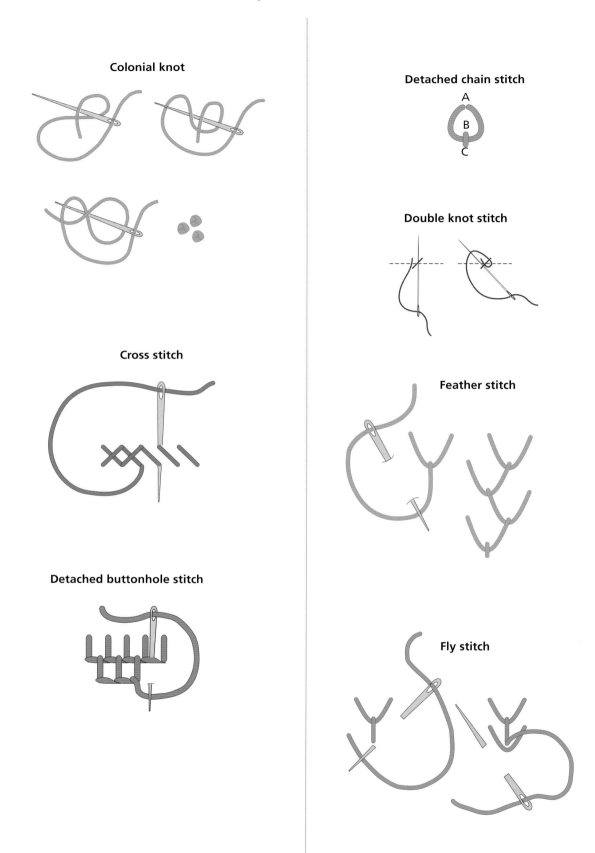

Colonial knot

Detached chain stitch

A

B

C

Double knot stitch

Cross stitch

Feather stitch

Detached buttonhole stitch

Fly stitch

French knot

Granitos stitch

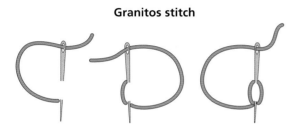

Herringbone stitch

Laid stitches anchored with a cross stitch

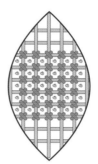
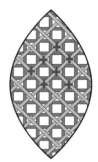

Leaf fly stitch

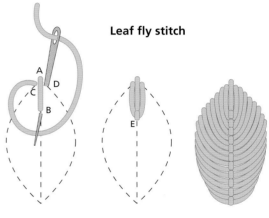

Long and short buttonhole stitch

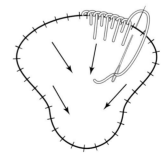

Long and short satin stitch

Spider stitch

Stem stitch/outline stitch

Pistil stitch

Straight stitch

Ribbon stitch

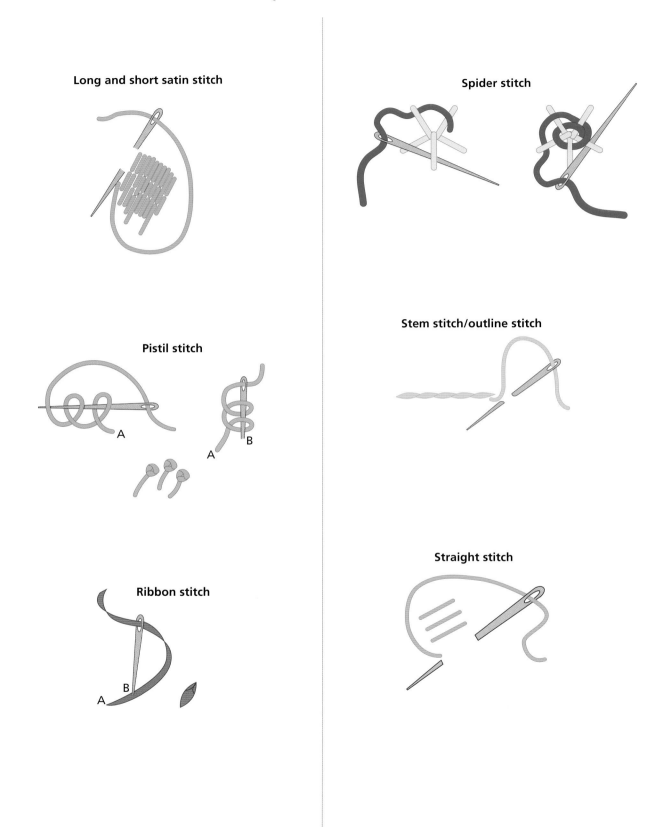

Turkey stitch

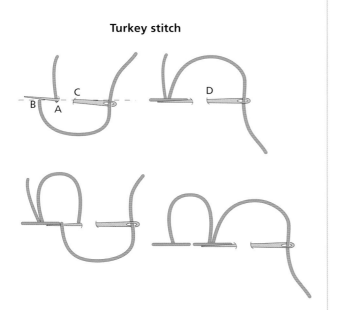

Whipped stem stitch

Wire couching

Whipped chain stitch

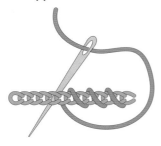

Acknowledgments

My students and friends are still my inspiration and they keep my brain ticking over to continue developing different and hopefully interesting projects to embroider.

My thanks go especially to Avril D'Arcy, a dear friend who found it hard to keep up with me as the book evolved and I frequently changed the contents list and the designs. Both she and Sandra Pedersen have given me support and encouragement when it all became too hard at times. I am particularly grateful to Sandra for embroidering the Cornucopia design so that I could use it for an evening bag and to Avril for her help in re-embroidering some of the designs in different colour combinations. We have had great fun on most Monday afternoons discussing these different versions.

I would like to thank my suppliers: Kaalund Yarns for creating such wonderful yarns and colours for me to work with; Robyn Alexander from Colour Streams; Semco Crafts for Anchor threads; and Maria George for some of the beads.

My thanks also go to my long-suffering husband for his support and understanding throughout the whole process.

Finally, I would like to dedicate this book to my Mum, who passed away while it was in progress. After I wrote the first book she said how proud she was of me (I was never an academic at school), and this gave me the motivation to finish this book — I am sure she would have really loved to see it.

Stockists

Some of these stockists are wholesalers only, but if you contact them they will give you the names of your nearest suppliers.

Sally Milner Publishing Pty Ltd
Address: PO Box 2104, Bowral, NSW 2576, Australia
Phone: +61 (0)2 4862 4212
Fax: +61 (0)2 4862 4214
Email: info@sallymilner.com.au
Website: http://www.sallymilner.com.au

THREADS
Anchor threads
From Semco Crafts Australia
Address: Unit 4, 7–11 Parraweena Road, Taren Point, NSW 2229, Australia
Phone: +61 (0)2 8543 4300; 1800 641 277 (tollfree within Australia)
Fax: +61 (0)2 9525 8887; 1800 624 155 (tollfree within Australia)
Email: info@semco.com.au
Website: http://www.semco.com.au

From Semco Crafts New Zealand
Address: 33c Sir William Avenue, East Tamaki, Auckland, New Zealand
Phone: +64 (0)9 273 8040
Fax: +64 (0)9 273 8041
Email: info@semco.com.au
Website: http://www.semco.com.au

Cascade House Australia
Address: 59 Albert Street, Creswick, VIC 3363, Australia
Phone/Fax: +61 (0)3 5345 1120
Email: cascade@cascadehouse.com.au
Website: http://www.cascadehouse.com.au

Colour Streams
Address: 5 Palm Ave, Mullumbimby, NSW 2472, Australia
Proprietor: Robyn Alexander
Phone/Fax: +61 (0)2 6684 2577
Email: colourstreams@colourstreams.com.au
Website: http://www.colourstreams.com.au

DMC Threads
Wholesaler in Australia: Radda Pty Ltd,
Address: 51–55 Carrington Road, Marrickville, NSW 2204, Australia; PO Box 317, Earlwood 2206, Australia
Phone: +61 (0)2 9559 3088
Fax: +61 (0)2 9559 5388
Email: cservice@radda.com.au

Ireland Needlecraft Pty Ltd
Distributor for The Caron Collection, The Thread Gatherer, Rainbow Gallery Crystal Rays, Mill Hill beads
Address: PO Box 1175, Narre Warren, VIC 3805, Australia
Phone: +61 (0)3 9702 3222
Fax: +61 (0)3 9702 3255
Email: enquiries@irelandneedlecraft.com.au

Kaalund Yarns
Address: PO Box 17, Banyo, QLD 4014, Australia
Director: Jean Inglis
Phone/Fax: +61 (0)7 3267 6266
Email: yarns@ kaalundyarns.com.au
Website: http//:kaalundyarns.com.au

UK supplier

The Viking Loom
Address: 22 High Petergate, York, YO1 7EH, UK
Phone/Fax: +44 9047 65599
Email: vikingloom@vikingloom.co.uk
Website: http://www.vikingloom.co.uk

Rainbow Silks
Address: 6 Wheelers Yard, High Street,
Great Missenden, Bucks HP16 OAL, UK
Phone: +44 (0)1494 862111
Fax: +44 (0)1494 862651
Email: caroline@rainbowsilks.co.uk
Website: http://www.rainbowsilks.co.uk

Ireland supplier

Madra Dubh Fabrics and Threads
Address: Madra Dubh House, Ballinaboola,
Co. Wexford, Ireland
Phone/Fax: +353 5142 8791
Email: madradubh@eircom.net

Needle Necessities
Address: Ben Britim Distributors, Vailima Scarlet
Street, Mittagong, NSW 2575
Phone: +61 (0)2 4871 2415
Email: benbri@bigpond.net.au
Website: For colour charts and distributors or
retailers outside Australia, see
http//www.needlenecessities.com

Rajmahal Art Silks
Address: 182 High Street, Kangaroo Flat,
VIC 3555, Australia
Phone: +61 (0)3 5447 7699
Fax: +61 (0)3 5447 7899
Email: rajinfo@ozemail.com.au
Website: http://www.rajmahal.com.au

YLI Silk Floss
Available from Cotton On Creations, Exclusive
Australian distributor for YLI Corporation and
Bear Threads Ltd.

Address: Unit 2, 52 Govetts Leap Road,
Blackheath, NSW 2785
Phone: +61 (0)2 4787 6588
Fax: +61 (0)2 4787 6544
Email: cottononcreations@bigpond.com.au.

BEADS

Maria George Pty Ltd
For Delica beads (especially satin mix), cut glass
beads in lustre colours, cut glass (faceted) beads,
Czech and Austrian crystals
Address: 179 Flinders Lane, Melbourne,
VIC 3000, Australia
Phone: +61 (0)3 9650 1151
Fax: +61 (0)3 9650 5318
Email: mariag@mariageorge.com.au
Website: http://mariageorge.com.au

Bead Trimming & Craft Co.
For crystals, crystal pearls and dark pink satin
beads for *Twisted vine*
Address: 39 Merivale Street, South Brisbane,
QLD 4101, Australia
Phone: +61 (0)7 3844 5722
Fax: +61 (0)7 3844 7999
Email: sales@beadtrimmingcraft.com.au
Website: http://www.beadtrimmingcraft.com.au

Photios Bros Pty Ltd
Address: 66 Druitt Street, Sydney, NSW 2000,
Australia
Phone: +61 (0)2 9267 1428
Fax: +61 (0)2 9267 1953

Creative Beadcraft Ltd (UK)
Address: Unit 2, Asheridge Road, Chesham,
Buckinghamshire HP5 2PT, UK
Phone: +44 (0)1494 778818
Fax: +44 (0)1494 718510
Email: tracey@cheddingtonbucks.freeserve.co.uk
Website: http://www.creativebeadcraft.co.uk

OTHER
Eliza Gallery
For framing
Address: Mornington Industrial Park, Mornington,
VIC 3931
Phone: +61 (0)3 5975 7343
Fax: +61 (0)3 5977 2717
Email: elizagal@artmaterials.com.au
Website: http://www.artmaterials.com.au

Lyn Spencer
Supplier in Australia for Santa head and hands
Address: 16 Sherwood Crescent, Dandenong,
VIC 3175, Australia
Phone: +61 (0)3 9774 7326

AUTHOR
Helan Pearce
Address: 22 Mather Road, Mt Eliza, VIC 3930,
Australia
Phone: +61 (0)3 9787 0963
Fax: +61 (0)3 9787 6207
Email: Helan_Pearce@connexus.net.au

Gold evening bag embroidered by Sandra Pedersen.
Cream and gold mask, trumpet flower, green evening bag, luxuriant leaves on a
hat box, tassels and Christmas cornucopia embroidered by Avril D'Arcy.